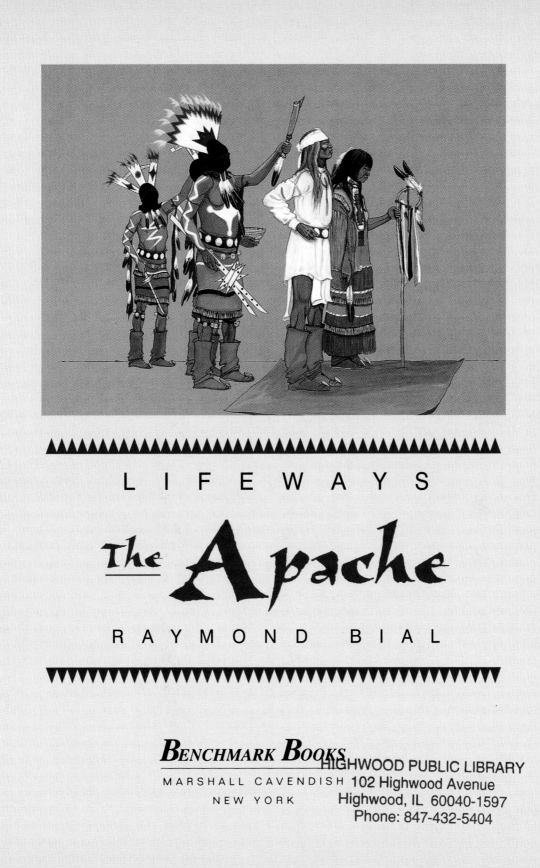

L I F E W A Y S

The Apache

R A Y M O N D   B I A L

BENCHMARK BOOKS

MARSHALL CAVENDISH
NEW YORK

SERIES CONSULTANT: JOHN BIERHORST

ACKNOWLEDGMENTS

This book would not have been possible without the assistance of a number of organizations and individuals, including many native people, who have devoted themselves to sustaining the traditions and enriching the contemporary life of the Apache in Arizona, New Mexico, and Oklahoma. I am especially indebted to the staff of the Apache Culture Center at Fort Apache for their gracious assistance. I would like to express my appreciation to the people of the Fort Apache Reservation for allowing me to make photographs there, along with the staff at Native Seeds/SEARCH in Tucson. I would like to thank the Northern Arizona University Archives, the National Archives, the Library of Congress, and the Philbrook Museum of Art for furnishing a number of illustrations.

   I would like to thank my editor Kate Nunn and her able assistant Doug Sanders for their hard work with *The Apache* and other titles in the Lifeways series. I am also very much indebted to John Bierhorst for his meticulous review of the manuscript and many helpful suggestions. Once again, I would like to express my deepest appreciation to my wife, Linda, and my children Anna, Sarah, and Luke for their cheerful support. It was especially delightful to travel on the photo assignment in Arizona in the company of my wife and children, and then finish the research and writing of this book in the midst of my family at home.

Benchmarks Books
Marshall Cavendish Corporation
99 White Plains Road, Tarrytown, New York 10591-9001
Text copyright © 2001 by Raymond Bial
Map copyright © 2001 by the Marshall Cavendish Corporation
Map by Rodica Prato

Library of Congress Cataloging-in-Publication Data
Bial, Raymond.
The Apache / Raymond Bial.
p. cm. — (Lifeways)
Includes bibliographical references and index.
Summary: Discusses the history, culture, beliefs, changing ways, and notable people of the Apache.
ISBN 0-7614-0939-4
1. Apache Indians—Juvenile literature. [1. Apache Indians.
2. Indians of North America—New Mexico.] I. Title.
E99.A6 B53 2001 979'.004972—dc21 99-044717
Printed in Italy
6 5 4 3

Cover photos: Raymond Bial

The photographs in this book are used by permission and through the courtesy of: The Philbrook Museum of Art, Tulsa, OK: 1, 44, 47, 67, 87. Raymond Bial, 6, 8-9, 12, 15,18, 21, 26-27, 30, 33, 36-37, 49, 53, 57, 58, 61, 70-71, 73, 76, 77, 78, 79, 82-83, 92-93, 94-95, 97, 98, 100-101. Library of Congress: 34, 55, 80-81. Museum of New Mexico: J. R. Riddle, 76160, 39; 38195, 41; Edward S. Curtis, 108112, 50; Edward S. Curtis, 2106, 63; T. Harmon Parkhurst, 3217, 90; Carl N. Werntz, 37422, 105; Ben Wittick, 15903, 115; 2109, 117. National Archives, 42, 89, 112.

This book is respectfully dedicated
to all the Apache peoples,
whose spirit of independence
I've long admired.

Contents

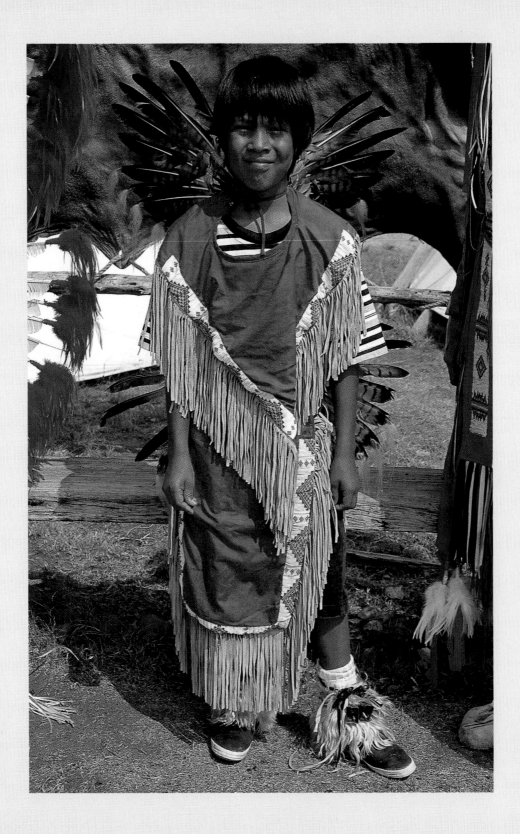

Author's Note

AT THE DAWN OF THE TWENTIETH CENTURY, NATIVE Americans were thought to be a vanishing race. However, despite four hundred years of warfare, deprivation, and disease, American Indians have not gone away. Countless thousands have lost their lives, but over the course of this century the populations of native tribes have grown tremendously. Even as American Indians struggle to adapt to modern Western life, they have also kept the flame of their traditions alive—the language, religion, stories, and the everyday ways of life. An exhilarating renaissance in Native American culture is now sweeping the nation from coast to coast.

The Lifeways books depict the social and cultural life of the major nations, from the early history of native peoples in North America to their present-day struggles for survival and dignity. Historical and contemporary photographs of traditional subjects, as well as period illustrations, are blended throughout each book so that readers may gain a sense of family life in a tipi, a hogan, or a longhouse.

No single book can comprehensively portray the intricate and varied lifeways of an entire tribe, or nation. I only hope that young people will come away with a deeper appreciation for the rich tapestry of Indian culture—both then and now—and a keen desire to learn more about these first Americans.

1. Origins

To the
Apache, the
land was
sacred,
including the
Superstition
Mountains
just east of
present-day
Phoenix,
Arizona.

EACH OF THE APACHE (uh-PATCH-ee) PEOPLES HAS A RICH AND INTRICATE system of beliefs expressed through stories of the creation of the earth and the appearance of the first humans. There are many versions of the story, but in each the Apaches emerged from a mystical under-world and came to live in the Southwest. To this day, the Apaches remain closely bound to this dry country of high mountains, jagged hills, and deep canyons, as well as sprawling deserts and dense forests of pine, cottonwood, juniper, and oak.

Here is a version of the story of how the world and the Jicarilla (HE-kuh-REE-yuh) Apache, a band that now lives in New Mexico, were created:

"The Origin of the Jicarilla Apache"

In the beginning, there was nothing—no ground, no earth, only darkness, water, and cyclones. There were no people, no living things, only the Hactcin (hasht-sheen), or holy people, who have been here forever. It was a lonely place. So, the Hactcin made the earth in the form of a living woman and called her Mother. They made the sky in the form of a man and called him Father.

The Hactcin lived in the underworld. The mountains had a Hactcin as a guardian spirit, as did each plant and fruit that came to grow there. Everything was perfect and holy in the underworld. The people of the underworld were not yet real, with flesh and blood. They lived as if in a dream; they were only shadows of themselves.

One day, the Black Hactcin, who was the most powerful, decided to create the animals. As the people watched, he fashioned a clay figure with four legs and a tail. The figure looked strange to them—until it began to walk. The people were amazed.

The Black Hactcin spoke to the clay figure, "You are all alone, which is not good. I will have others come from your body." With his great power, the Black Hactcin caused all sorts of animals of the land to emerge from the body of the creature. Even the Black Hactcin was amazed at the great variety of animals, each with its own distinctive appearance and habits. The Jicarilla still delight in these animals that walk or fly about the earth—some with hair, horns, and hooves, others with scales.

At that time, all the animals could speak the Jicarilla language, and they asked the Black Hactcin where they should make their home. He told them to spread across the land—the mountains, deserts, and plains—and to live in the place that best suited their nature.

After he had created the animals of the land, the Black Hactcin held out his hand and asked for water. A drop of rain fell into his open palm. He mixed the drop with earth and shaped a bird from the mud. "Now use those wings to fly," he said.

The mud figure instantly came to life and flew through the sky, but soon the bird became lonely. He flew in each of the four directions—east, south, west, and north—then came back and told the Black Hactcin, "I can find no other birds."

So, the Black Hactcin whirled the bird around and around. The bird glimpsed many images flashing past him—hawks, eagles, songbirds. These blurred pictures then turned into living birds, which

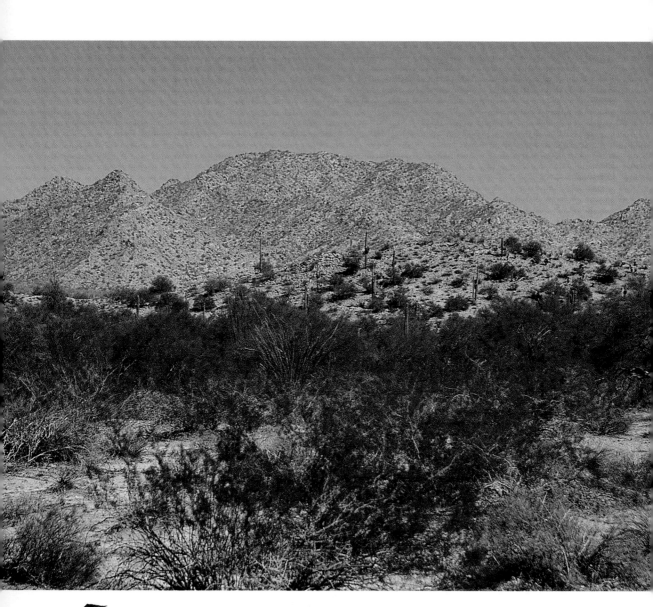

*T*he Apache made their home in the rugged land of the American Southwest, much of which was arid desert country.

circled the sky. And to this day, birds prefer the air, seldom lighting upon the ground, because that first drop of water came from the sky.

The birds then came to the Black Hactcin and asked, "Where shall we live? Where shall we rest?"

The Black Hactcin told them to fly in all directions and then come back to tell him which place they liked best. "You may have that place as your home."

"What should we eat?" the birds next asked.

The Black Hactcin raised his hand east, south, west, and north, and all kinds of seeds fell upon the ground. When the birds went to eat them, the seeds turned into worms, grasshoppers, and many other insects.

The Black Hactcin then told Turkey, "You will be in charge of all these seeds." And this is why the Jicarilla honor this bird's feathers, placing one in each corner of their fields when they plant their crops. The turkey is also striped like Indian corn with a head like a corn tassel. In fact, every part of the turkey's body represents some part of the corn plant.

The Black Hactcin next took moss from the river's edge, rolling it in his hands. When he threw the moss into the water, it turned into fish, frogs, and all the other creatures that live in the water. When the birds flew over the river, some of their feathers dropped into the water and turned into ducks, herons, cranes, and other waterbirds.

Now the animals and birds had everything, or so the Black Hactcin thought. But the creatures came together in council and told the powerful spirit, "We need another companion. We need people."

"Why do you need others?" the Black Hactcin asked.

"Because you will not always be with us. You will go away from time to time."

The Black Hactcin agreed. "Perhaps someday I will go to a place where you will not see me."

He asked the animals and birds to gather materials from nature, including corn pollen and precious stones. He then instructed them to remain a short distance away from him as he turned to the east, south, west, and north. With corn pollen, he next traced an outline on the ground, just like his own body. He placed the precious stones within the figure and they became flesh and bone—veins of turquoise, blood of red ocher, bones of white rock, bone marrow of white clay, skin of coral, eyes of abalone, pupils of jet, and fingernails and teeth of opal.

The Black Hactcin blew wind into the man and he came to life, the path of the wind marked in the whorls of his fingertips. Noisily pushing forward, the birds and animals were eager to see the man.

The Black Hactcin then instructed the man how to stand up, walk, and run, as well as how to speak, laugh, and shout. When the birds first glimpsed the man they were so happy they sang as though it were dawn. To this day, at the girl's puberty rite, a man runs in four clockwise circles, as he was once directed by the Black Hactcin, and an old woman makes a chirping noise in her ear.

The man was able to speak with the animals and birds, but otherwise he was alone. So the animals and birds asked the Black Hactcin to help the man. That night the man's eyes became heavy,

*W*andering over the dry land, Apache bands often sought water in springs and streams cutting through deep ravines.

and he fell asleep. He dreamed long and deep about a young woman, and when he awoke she was sitting beside him.

"Let us speak together," the man suggested. And they did. Then they walked and ran laughing together. The birds made sweet music so the couple would continue to be happy together.

And this is how the earth and all its creatures and the first two people came to be.

LIKE OTHER NATIVE PEOPLES OF NORTH AMERICA, THE ANCESTORS OF THE Apaches were hunters and gatherers who made their way across the Bering Strait over a narrow land bridge that joined Asia and North America thousands of years ago. It may have been 12,000 years ago, but some scientists now think that Asian people first migrated to North America between 28,000 and 38,000 years ago. The Apache ancestors, known as the Athapascans, are believed to be one of the last groups to cross this land bridge during the last ice age. For thousands of years they lived in an area that is now Alaska and the Canadian Northwest, speaking the same Athapascan language as the other tribes living there. Dressed in animal skins, they hunted mammoths and giant bison, along with deer and other small animals.

Sometime after A.D. 1000, most likely between the thirteenth and sixteenth centuries, Apachean people migrated southward along the eastern slopes of the Rocky Mountains into the American Southwest. At that time, the climate of the Southwest was cooler and wetter than it is today, and the land was covered with vast grasslands and lines of trees along the riverbeds. The people adapted to their new world and formed a deep bond with the land that provided them with food, clothing, and shelter. Along with game and wild plants, they learned where to find water, stones suitable for weapons and tools, and wood for their fires.

Much of the Apachean past remains a mystery. Why, after thousands of years in the cold North, did they abandon their snowshoes and travel all the way to the Southwest? Are their homes, called wickiups (WIK-ee-ups), based on the small huts made by Northwest Indians? Why are the Apacheans of the Southwest so far removed from their Athapascan relatives in Canada and Alaska? It is believed that most of the people came in a large, single migration to an area near Gobernador Canyon in northwest New Mexico. Apache stories of origin place their emergence around this area. Small bands of hunters and their families followed over the next several generations.

At the time of their migration, the Southwest was home to several flourishing native civilizations, including the Anasazi and the Hohokam. It was once thought that the Apacheans drove these peoples from their homes. However, when the Apachean people arrived in the Four Corners region (where the borders of Colorado, Utah, New Mexico, and Arizona meet), they most likely found that the Anasazi had already relocated to villages in the upper Rio Grande valley in present-day New Mexico. The Hohokam of southern Arizona had also abandoned their ancestral settlements. Today the descendants of the Anasazi are known as the Pueblo; and the inheritors of the Hohokam territory are the Tohono O'odham (also called Papago) and the Pima.

Later, as their way of life changed, the Apacheans drifted into two distinct groups: the Apache and the Navajo. The Navajo settled as farmers in the Four Corners area while the restless Apache spread over three desert regions—the Great Basin, Sonoran, and Chihuahuan. Over time, they scattered farther into what are now southeastern Colorado, Arizona, eastward into present-day central and south Texas, and into northern Mexico. *Apache* probably came from the Zuñi word *Apachu* meaning "enemy." However, the Apache refer to themselves as *Ndee* (in-DAY), which in their language means "people."

A varied land, the Apachería featured mountains, meadows, and the low grasslands that bordered the rugged desert terrain.

Hardy and clever, the Apaches thrived in the Southwest. They made weapons and tools from wood and stone. While the men hunted, the women gathered berries, nuts, and seeds. Whatever they needed they learned to make with their own hands. Artful raiders as well as able warriors, from the time the Apaches arrived in the Southwest they plundered the storehouses of the neighboring Pueblos, who grew corn, beans, and squash. Although they occasionally traded with the Pueblos, the Apache did not enjoy good relations with their neighbors and, unlike the Navajo, were not heavily influenced by the Pueblos. Although relative newcomers to the Southwest, they were well established in their new home country long before the Spanish, Mexicans, and Anglo-Americans ventured into the region.

Never united as a single nation, the Apache preferred to live in scattered bands, sometimes fighting with each other. Over the generations, they drifted into several tribes, which came to speak their own dialects, and many smaller groups. In addition to the Navajos, the principal Apachean-speaking peoples came to be: the Chiricahua, Jicarilla, Lipan, Mescalero, and Western Apache. The Chiricahua were divided into three bands: the Central and Southern band, and the Eastern band whose range joined that of the Mescalero. The Jicarilla were given this name by the Spanish because of their basket-making skills. *Mescaleros*, or "mescal makers," were so named because mescal from the century plant was the band's favorite food. The Lipan Apache made their home in Texas, while the Western Apaches divided into distinctive groups: Northern Tonto, Southern

Tonto, Cibecue, White Mountain, and San Carlos. There is also a small band of Yavapai (YAV-uh-pie) Apaches in western Arizona.

When they first encountered people of European descent, the Apache were wandering the rugged landscape of eastern Arizona, New Mexico, western Oklahoma and Texas, southeastern Colorado, and western Kansas, as well as parts of Mexico. Those who lived in the eastern portion of this territory, at the edges of the Great Plains—the Jicarilla, Mescalero, Lipan, and Kiowa-Apache—adopted the lifeways of the Plains Indians. They became skilled horsemen, lived in tipis, and hunted buffalo, while the Chiricahua and Western Apache continued as hunters and gatherers. From the Pueblo, they also learned to grow corn and melons, and later pumpkins, beans, and squash.

Skillful warriors and raiders, the Apache were feared by the Pueblo and the Spanish and Anglo settlers who crossed their territory. Viewing the Spanish and Anglos as intruders, the Apaches courageously resisted having their lands taken away, even after New Mexico was annexed by the United States in 1846. Heroic leaders such as Cochise and Geronimo, both of whom were Chiricahua Apaches, battled U.S. forces for several decades.

The People and the Land

The vast deserts and mountain ranges of the Apache homeland is known as Apachería. This region stretches from south Texas to central Arizona, and from northern Mexico to the High Plains of eastern Colorado. When the Apache acquired horses sometime after

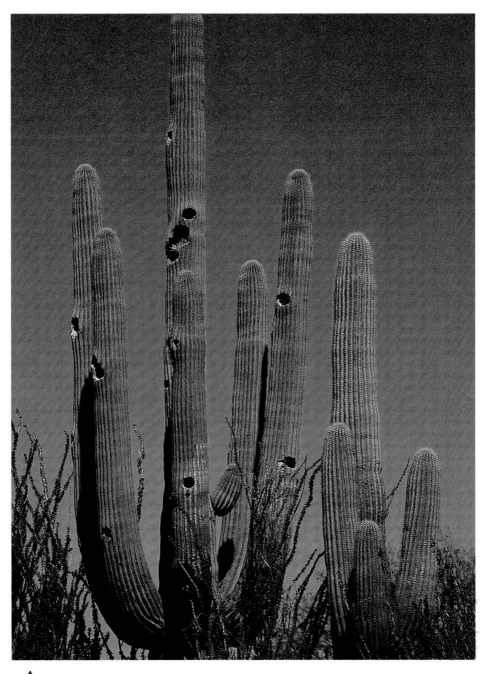

A *symbol of the desert, these saguaros tower over the scrubby brush.*

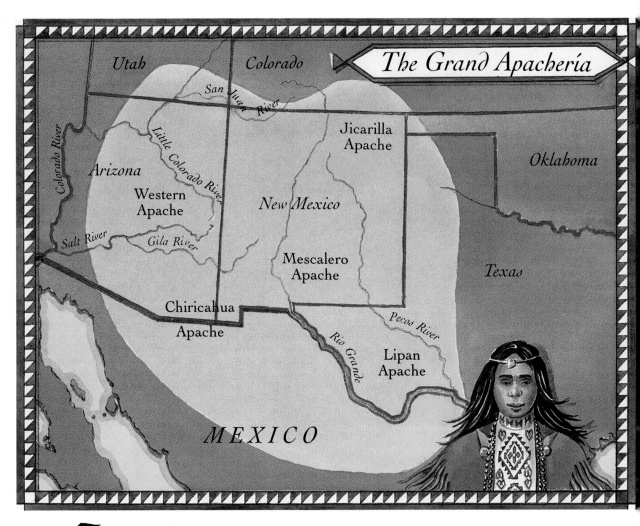

The Grand Apacheria

The Apachería, also known as the Grand Apachería, was a vast tract of land the Apache once roamed without restriction.

1620, bands began to spread over the plains east of the Guadalupe Mountains in southern New Mexico and southwestern Texas. This was a land of brittle grass and small rugged trees called mesquite. Here, the Apache followed the enormous herds of buffalo. About

1718, they were defeated by the Comanches and withdrew to the western edges of the dry grasslands. Some Apache bands joined with the Kiowa in the central plains near the confluence of the Platte and Missouri Rivers and became known as the Kiowa-Apaches. They settled far from the Spanish but later found themselves directly in the path of American settlers pushing westward. Other Apaches, who came to be known as the Lipan Apaches, remained in Texas, where they continued to hunt buffalo and live in tipis.

The Jicarilla Apaches eventually moved to the mountainous regions of present-day northern New Mexico near the Rio Grande. The Mescalero Apaches ranged in the desert country of New Mexico, south of Jicarilla territory as far as El Paso del Norte on the lower Rio Grande. Here, they battled for survival in a hot climate and rocky, parched terrain. They traded with the Spanish or raided their villages until about 1775 when they finally entered into a peace agreement. Serving as scouts and living among the Spanish, they soon learned their language and adopted many of their customs and clothing styles.

The Apache who lived in Arizona included the Western Apaches and the Chiricahua, who historically wandered the seemingly endless stretches of desert in the southeastern part of the state. Here, the Chiracahuas made their way along arroyos, or gullies, followed the trails of deer and small wild pigs known as javelina, and climbed the forested mountains that rose abruptly from the desert floor. This land was laced with canyons and marked by unusual rock formations. Unlike many wandering peoples who were forced to live on marginal lands, the Apache chose to roam the rugged mountains and deserts because they loved this land and their nomadic way of life. This was a place of jackrabbits and coyotes, lizards and snakes, as well as numerous varieties of birds, including eagles, hawks, and owls. Every cactus had painful needles, just as rattlesnakes, coiled beneath the rocks, flashed their fangs, and scorpions threatened with their sting.

Suffering hunger and thirst, extreme heat and cold, the Apache battled for survival. In this land of deserts and ancient mountains, they endured the terrain and the climate, going days without water and eating wood rats or lizards when they could find no other food. To the Apache, every stranger was a potential enemy. In the American Southwest and deeper into Mexico, they skillfully eluded both Mexican and U.S. soldiers in their quest to keep the freedom they so deeply cherished.

Farther north, the Western Apache favored a cool climate and wooded mountains. They made their home—and continue to live—in the high plateau country of the White Mountains, well above the stately saguaros and other cactus. Here, there were ponderosa pines, deep blue lakes, and aspens shimmering in the breeze, as well as rushing streams and springs of clear water. The Western Apache homeland extended south of the present-day city of Flagstaff, Arizona, along the Verde River, across a ridge called the Mogollon Rim, into the beautiful White Mountains down through the Salt River canyon all the way to New Mexico. Their range included the Gila River valley and parts of the Salt River canyon to the Santa Catalina

Mountains, on to the Pinaleño Mountains, as far south as the tip of the San Pedro River valley in northern Mexico. The Western Apache hunted deer in the forests and meadows and caught beaver along the streams.

As they still do today, the Apache gathered the hearts of agave, or mescal, to bake over hot rocks. They also ate cactus fruits, acorns, pine nuts, and walnuts, and raised corn, beans, and other crops. Wherever they lived, the Apaches loved the land, plants, and animals that provided them with food, clothing, and shelter. Despite the often difficult conditions, their keen knowledge and skill enable them to thrive. They also came to be bound spiritually to their land of mountains and valleys, deserts and canyons, grasslands and forests of ponderosa pine, juniper, and quaking aspens.

the Deserts and Mountains

The Apache lived in small homes called wickiups, which could be easily constructed wherever they decided to make camp.

UNTIL THE APACHES ENCOUNTERED SPANISH EXPLORERS, MEXICAN soldiers, and later United States forces, they roamed freely within their home territory. When they broke camp, the women packed their belongings, and when they set up the next camp, the women built another wickiup, a small dome-shaped hut covered with brush, thatch, or animal skins. Hunters, gatherers, and occasionally farmers, the people knew the land intimately—where they might find water, where they had previously hidden food, and where they might pick some nourishing berries. The Western Apache planted corn and other crops, but the harvests were not always bountiful, so the men hunted deer, rabbits, turkeys, and other game while the women gathered cactus fruit and acorns.

The Apache loved raiding and warfare, and from an early age boys were taught to be warriors. They learned to remain absolutely silent as they made their way across the land, raiding villages or avenging a death. Then they would go without sleep as they stood guard all night. They learned to send and read smoke signals. When the boys were about fifteen years old, they were ready for raids and warfare.

From their mothers, girls learned to do the household chores—cooking and caring for the children. When they came of age, they underwent a puberty rite known as the Sunrise Ceremony. In this joyous event, girls danced for four days to the beat of water drums and songs. They were blessed in sacred rituals and honored for the strength they would need as wives and mothers.

Apaches learned to be tough—they often went for long stretches without food or water, walking up to seventy miles a day in the searing heat. Wherever the Apache journeyed, they carried within themselves an abiding respect for the land. This Apache song speaks of their regard for the land:

> *Far on the desert ridges stands the cactus*
> *Lo, the blossoms swaying*
> *To and fro the blossoms swaying, swaying*

Wickiups

Tribes lived in several kinds of houses. The Lipan Apache, Kiowa-Apache, and several Jicarilla bands lived in tipis, like other Plains Indians. These cone-shaped homes were made of wooden poles lashed together at the top with rawhide and covered with tanned buffalo hides. A few Jicarilla lived in adobe homes like the Pueblos of New Mexico and Arizona. Like the Navajo, other Apache lived in earth-covered dwellings called hogans.

However, most tribes, including the Mescalero, Chiricahua, Western Apache, and many Jicarilla lived in wickiups. To make a wickiup, women set mesquite, willow, or cottonwood poles in a circle of shallow holes, bent the tops over, and tied them together with strips of yucca leaf. On this frame they tied bunches of bear grass with yucca string, one overlapping the other to shed the rain. During cold or rainy weather, the women covered the frames with animal skins. In later years, the Apache traded for canvas which they used to waterproof their dwellings.

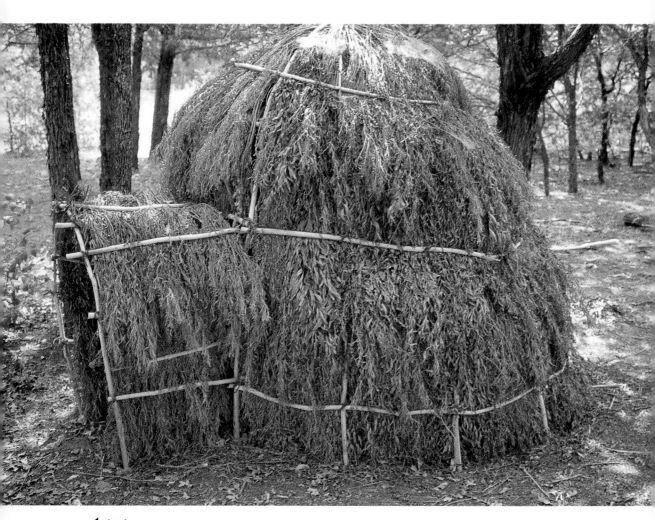

Wickiups sheltered entire families from the intense heat of the desert sun, as well as occasional rain and cold.

The women left a small hole in the top to vent the smoke that rose from the fire burning in a shallow pit in the center of the floor. There was also a low doorway, facing east toward the rising sun, which the Apaches considered the sacred direction. To keep out the wind and cold, women covered the doorway with a skin or blanket. There was no floor, just the hard-packed earth, which the women swept clean. About 7 feet tall, wickiups ranged from 8 to 15 feet in diameter. Smaller than tipis, they could still house a large family—parents and their children, as well as grandparents, aunts, and uncles. Easily set up and taken down, as well as transported to the next camp, wickiups were ideal dwellings for a people who moved sometimes as often as every two weeks.

During the warm summers, the family moved outside and lived in a circular brush windbreak. Women also made brush shades, or ramadas. They set posts in the ground in a rectangle, tied branches horizontally to the posts to brace the structure, and then wove twigs and brush into the frame, making a kind of latticework. Under the shade, shielded from the baking sun, women cooked, wove baskets, and did other household chores.

Because they moved so often, the Apache had few possessions. Beds were made with pole frames, cushioned with dry grass and perhaps a blanket. Women also had baskets, water jugs, and pounding stones and stone slabs for grinding nuts, seeds, and corn. In later years, they might also have and iron cooking pot, skillet, or dishpan, which they had acquired through trade.

Families, Bands, and Camps

The Apache preferred to live independently in small bands. Historically, they had no central tribal government and did not even come together as a tribe for ceremonies, such as the Sun Dance celebrated by many Plains Indians. Because the arid land could not provide enough food for large groups of people, the Apache lived in scattered bands, composed of several extended families, or "family clusters," each with its own territory for hunting, gathering, and farming. Among the Western Apache, society was and still is based upon a system of clans rather than families. Every person is born into a clan. Today, there are sixty-two different clans.

The Apache were matrilocal, or centered on the mother's home. Throughout their lives, daughters usually remained with their mother's band. When a couple married, the husband went to live with his bride's family in a nearby wickiup. As with the Navajo, to insure harmony in the marriage, the Apache husband and mother-in-law did not speak or look at each other. If the couple ever separated or one of them died, their children remained with the mother's family. The Apache were also matrilineal, meaning family descent was based on the mother's family—except for the Chiracahua who trace both sides of the family. The wife's grandmother was highly esteemed within the family. She traditionally wielded a great deal of authority.

Living in camps, extended families formed the basis of social and political life among the Apache. These families, which included the older parents, unmarried children, and several married daughters

*M*any families still build shelters known as shades in their backyards. There, women weave baskets and sometimes cook meals.

and their families, usually formed four or five households. Each family had a headman who instilled discipline in his group, insuring that everyone rose early and worked hard. From two to six families joined together to form bands based on blood relations or marriage, or simply because they inhabited the same region.

Each band also had a leader, or chief, who inherited the position or was chosen for his ability to provide for the people through hunting and raiding. Yet the chief lacked authority to punish anyone,

In their desert camp, these Apache women and their children gather in front of two wickiups.

so his role was largely advisory. However, among the Apache, social disapproval was a powerful force in maintaining order. The difficult terrain and the threat of hunger also bound the people closely together. Cooperation was essential if they were going to survive as they wandered the landscape of sharp rocks and hot sand. Protection was essential too. It was unsafe for a woman to gather seeds by herself—she might be attacked by an enemy or wild animal. Other work, such as gathering and baking mescal, required many hands. Men rarely hunted alone, in case of an accident or attack. So it became customary, even essential, for people to work together and share the bounty of the harvest and the hunt—their fate and fortune depended upon the group, not the individual.

Among the different bands, the chiefs were considered equal, but some enjoyed more respect due to their bravery as warriors, their skill as raiders, or their spiritual powers. Several times during the year, the chiefs led their bands to a gathering of the groups that journeyed in the same region or were related by marriage, custom, or dialect. These bands viewed themselves as members of the same tribe, but they never united as a nation. Even when faced by the Comanche onslaught, the Apaches on the southern Plains preferred to live and fight separately, which resulted in their being driven into New Mexico. Yet this nomadic way of life also made it nearly impossible for the Spanish, Mexicans, and the United States military to dominate the Apaches. Because the intruders had to deal with so many elusive, fiercely independent bands, it was difficult to place the Apache under their control.

3.Lifeways

Carefully woven, Apache baskets are known for their intricate designs.

EACH WICKIUP HOUSED THE PARENTS AND THEIR CHILDREN. TWO MARRIED couples rarely lived together in the same dwelling. Camps were made up of several clusters of wickiups, the number depending on how many married daughters were in the band. About twelve to twenty people lived in each band. The Apache have long been very social— one never sees a wickiup standing alone by itself. A man avoided camping alone, which despite his courage as a hunter and warrior, could have been a distressing, if not frightening, experience. The Apache were accustomed to living with their families, and they enjoyed and needed the company of others within the band.

Cycle of Life

Birth. Among the Western Apache, an expectant mother wore a maternity belt made of the skins of deer, mountain lion, and pronghorn antelope, since these animals were believed to have little difficulty in giving birth. Medicine men traditionally conducted rituals at the time of birth, but in more recent times, the mother was attended by a midwife. To wash the baby, the midwife squirted it with water she had warmed in her mouth. Then she rubbed the baby dry with grass, moss, or cloth and sprinkled it with cattail pollen. A few days later, a medicine sing was held at which the child was named.

A cradleboard was made, usually of pliable willow, oak, ash, or peeled mesquite root, with a hood to protect the baby's head. The wood frame was padded with moss, shredded bark, or strips of cloth. The Apache often said the baby was placed in the cradleboard "amid much sprinkling of pollen and praying to the gods." To amuse the baby and bring good fortune, small charms such as bags of pollen,

𝐼n this photograph by J. R. Riddle, a Mescalero Apache woman poses with her baby securely wrapped in a cradleboard on her back.

squirrel tails, pinecones, or stone arrowheads were hung from the hood. Chiricahua mothers hung badger paws to protect the baby from fear and cholla wood to prevent colds.

Childhood. From an early age children were taught to cooperate and contribute to the good of the family and the band. Children were loved and cherished by their parents and everyone else in the band, yet they were expected to be tough and strong. They had to be if they were going to survive the rigors of the Apache way of life.

Every day, even in winter, boys rose well before daybreak and swam in a nearby stream. To harden them against the cold, they sometimes had to roll naked in the snow. Each day, they also ran to the top of a hill and back carrying a mouthful of water to make sure they breathed through their nostrils. Girls also swam and ran to strengthen themselves. Many were as fast and as powerful as the boys. Working beside their mothers and the other women in the camp, girls also learned to work hard without complaint.

From the age of eight or nine, boys were already hunting with bows and arrows, proudly bringing home cottontail rabbits and squirrels. Apache boys were raised to become good hunters and fierce warriors. Both training and games sharpened their wits, made them skilled with weapons, and instilled in them courage, strength, and endurance.

Coming-of-Age. When his training was complete, a young man was allowed to go on his first raid. If he proved himself after four

*P*hotographed in 1866 at Fort Sumner, New Mexico, this Apache boy has begun to learn the skills needed to become a hunter and warrior.

From an early age, Apache girls were prepared for the important roles they would play in their families and communities.

raids, he was considered a man and could join the war parties. If he failed, he was scorned by the band. Young men could not marry until they had shown they could provide for their families by taking part in at least four raids. By this time, they were usually between twenty and twenty-five years old. When she could undertake all the household duties of a woman, generally between the ages of fifteen and eighteen, an Apache girl was deemed ready for marriage.

Marriage. Marriages were usually arranged by the young man's parents, after which the couples courted—although young people sometimes chose their own mate. Unmarried women were carefully watched by their relatives, but young people found a way to meet at ceremonies. When a young man wished to marry, he asked a relative, often an old woman, to approach the woman's family. If his offer was accepted, the young man presented her family with gifts—horses, blankets, or guns. The bride's family then presented a smaller number of gifts to his family.

The Apache did not have a wedding ceremony. A dwelling was built near the wickiup of the woman's parents, and the young man simply went to live in his new wife's camp. The couple lived in their own wickiup with the doorway facing away from the parent's home, out of respect for the long-standing taboo that a man should never look at and talk to his mother-in-law. It was believed that this practice eliminated the possibility of conflict and insured harmony between the households. The man was also expected to help support his wife's parents, although he did not neglect his own mother and father.

Death. Like the Navajo, the Apache dreaded the ghosts of the dead. They seldom spoke of the deceased, and then only acknowledged, "He is gone." Fearing that they might catch a disease from looking at a dead person or touching his possessions, people promptly buried the dead or placed the body in caves or clefts between rocks. The Western Apache wrapped their dead in blankets, and as a prayer that the dead person might safely journey to *Yaa ka'yu*, or heaven, they sprinkled ashes and pollen in a circle around the grave.

The family either buried or burned the possessions of the deceased and destroyed his wickiup. They believed the deceased might return for his belongings and bring the "ghost sickness," which

*E*ntitled Apache Baby Burial, *this 1948 watercolor by Allan Houser, a Chiracahua Apache, depicts a couple mourning the loss of their child.*

meant death for others in the band. Only a few people attended the burial, and afterward they burned their own clothing. The location of the grave was never mentioned, and if one had to speak of a dead relative, the person was referred to as the "one who used to be called..." then adding the deceased's name.

After a death, children's names were changed if the deceased had called them by those names. The band then moved to another camp, and it was forbidden to speak the name of the dead relative.

Hunting and Gathering

When they acquired horses in the late 1600s, the Jicarilla, Kiowa-Apache, Mescalero, and Lipan Apache began to hunt buffalo on horseback like the Plains Indians. The buffalo quickly became their primary source of meat, clothing, and shelter. The Western Apache and Chiricahuas—and the Mescaleros when they migrated to New Mexico—hunted many kinds of animals, especially deer, but also pronghorn antelope, elk, and mountain sheep and goats when they could get close enough to shoot them. They also caught and ate small animals, including opossums, wood rats, and cottontail rabbits—but few liked to eat the jackrabbit whose meat was considered tough and stringy. However, when food was scarce, people survived on just about any creature they could find.

Some tribes hunted wild turkeys and quail for food. They captured hawks, eagles, and turkeys for their feathers, which were used in rituals, on arrows, and occasionally in headdresses. Some Apaches avoided bears, believing that the spirits of evil people dwelled in them. Others hunted the powerful creatures not only for their flesh and fur, but for grease used in oiling guns and grooming hair. Mountain lions were killed whenever possible, not so much for the meat, but because the skins made excellent quivers. Badger, beaver, and otter were also hunted for their fur.

Occasionally, women and children joined in what was called a "surround hunt." Everyone formed a huge circle and walked slowly toward the middle. Cottontails and other small animals were clubbed as they tried to escape the tightening ring. However, the men most often went on hunting journeys in small groups. Before the hunt they fasted, because the spirits looked favorably on those in need. Deer was their favorite game, and they had to be excellent stalkers, as well as highly skilled with bow and arrow, to approach and bring down these wary animals. Sometimes, they smeared themselves with grease to disguise their odor and wore deer-head masks as they quietly stalked their prey. They never boasted of their skill or brought along baskets for carrying the meat back to camp, because they believed such arrogance resulted in bad luck. When they made a kill, they respected the animal as a gift of nature—not as an indication of their hunting ability. When they returned to camp, they were expected to share the meat with others. Fresh venison and other meats were roasted over the fire or boiled in various stews. Deer, elk, and buffalo meat was also cut into thin strips, hung over bushes to dry in the sun, then pounded and stored in leather bags.

Through each season, women gathered century plant, cactus fruit, grapes, acorns, pine nuts, mesquite pods, and walnuts, as well

In this 1947 watercolor by Allan Houser entitled Hunting Song, *a man offers thanks to the animals that help sustain him.*

as a variety of other berries, seeds, nuts, and roots. During the early spring, the Chiricahua and other Apache tribes gathered the tender green stems of the yucca plant, which they roasted for a day, sun-dried, and stored. Later, the stems would be soaked in water to soften them before they were eaten. Next the Apache harvested the white rootstocks and shoots of tule plants, which they boiled with meat to make a hearty soup. Later in the season, they picked the white blossoms of the narrow-leafed yucca and boiled them with meat or bones. Then long trips were made and camps set up to harvest the century plant, or mescal. In early summer, women harvested the blossoms of locust trees and picked wild onions.

By midsummer, they were collecting seeds and berries, as well as wild grapes. They journeyed to the desert in July to harvest the fruit of the saguaro cactus and collect the bean pods of the locust tree. In late summer, they went into the mountains to gather chokeberries, which they dried and stored, and to dig potatoes, which they stored in caves. Other autumn bounty included screw beans, broadleaf yucca fruit, prickly-pear cactus fruit, and mesquite beans, which were ground into flour for pancakes. There were also plenty of walnuts, piñon nuts, and acorns. The acorns were mixed with deer jerky and fat, then rolled into balls and stored as a kind of pemmican, an emergency food. At the end of the year, women picked the seeds of grasses. The Apache loved wild honey. The bees were forced out of the hive with smoke, or men laid skins on the ground and shot arrows until chunks of the comb broke off and fell down. The honey was squeezed into leather pouches. During the winter, the Apache

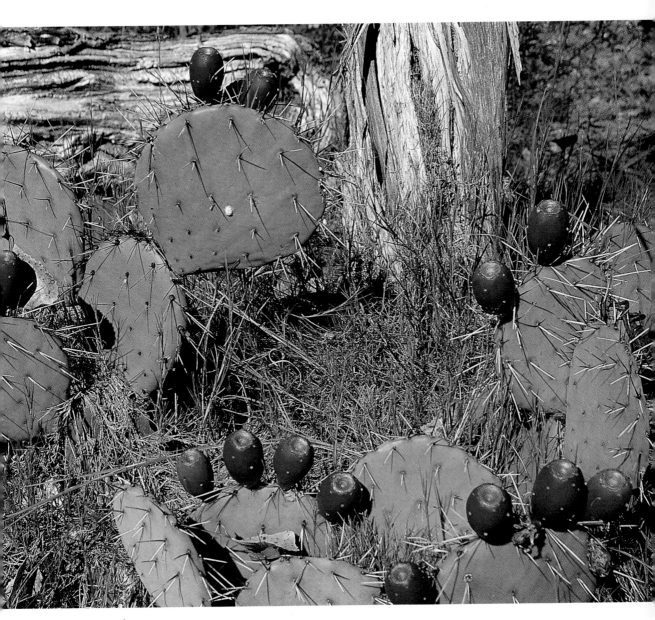

Apache women journeyed deep into the desert to harvest cactus fruit.

generally lived on stored vegetables, fruits, nuts, and meat until mid-spring when they could begin harvesting again.

Mescal from the agave plant was an especially important traditional food not only among the Mescaleros, but nearly all Apache tribes. It remains popular to this day. Harvesting mescal in May and June before the flowers bloomed, women cut the entire head or crown from the center of the plant. To bake the mescal, they built a

In this Edward Curtis photograph entitled Mescal Harvest, *an Apache woman gathers mescal in the desert.*

fire in a pit lined with stones. When the fire had burned down to hot coals, they laid down wet twigs, rushes, and grass, then piled the heads atop the smoking mass and covered them with more wet grass and twigs and a layer of soil. They built another fire over the pit and baked the heads from one to four days to make the sticky and syrupy food with a flavor like molasses. Dried in thin layers, mescal kept for a long time and provided the Apache with tasty, nutritious food during long journeys.

Green corn was boiled or roasted over the fire. The hard kernels of mature corn were ground into a coarse meal that was used to make pone and pancakes. The Western Apache also made a kind of beer from corn that they called *tulapai*.

Many of these foods were cached, or stored, in clay pots, which were hidden in caves or holes in the ground. They were left there until needed during the lean winter or when the band moved on to the next place. When traveling in dangerous territory women kept food bags and water jars filled in case they had to flee during the night. Individuals also carried small supplies of food attached to a belt.

Recipes

The Apaches roasted, baked, and boiled a wide variety of foods from plants and animals to make breads, soups, stews, and other dishes. These two recipes, which complement each other very well, have been recommended by the fifth grade class of the Cradleboard Elementary School in Fort Apache, Arizona. Today, fry bread is popular among many Native Americans.

Fry Bread

Ingredients

4 cups flour
½ teaspoon salt
1 tablespoon baking powder
Lard or shortening
1½ cups water

Combine all the ingredients, except the lard or shortening. Add about 1½ cups lukewarm water and knead until the dough is soft but not sticky. Shape dough into balls about the size of a small peach. Press the dough balls into patties about ½ inch thick. Fry the patties one at a time in about 1 inch of hot lard or shortening in a heavy pan until brown on both sides. Remove the fry bread, drain on paper towels, and serve hot with honey or jam.

If you'd like to make an "Indian Taco" instead, simply add beans, tomatoes, onions, cheese, and salsa on top.

With this favorite Apache dish, you might need to use beef instead of elk or deer, and whole wheat instead of acorn flour.

Acorn Stew

Ingredients

2½ to 3 pounds round steak (elk, deer, or beef) cut into bite-size pieces
Small acorns (enough to make ¾ cup of acorn flour) or ¾ cup of wheat flour
Salt

Simmer round steak in about one quart of water for three hours, or until meat is tender. Salt to taste. Shell and grind acorns into very fine flour until you have about ¾ cup of flour—or simply measure ¾ cup of wheat flour. Remove the meat from the pot, reserving the broth for later use. Shred the meat and mix with the flour in a large bowl. (Note: metal utensils or bowls will discolor acorn flour) Pour hot broth over the mixture, stir thoroughly, and serve in bowls with fry bread.

Clothing and Jewelry

Women prepared the skins of deer, antelope, elk, and buffalo. If the hair was to be removed, they buried the skin for a few days in moist soil, then soaked it in warm water, stretched it over a pole, and removed it with a dull knife. With a sharp knife, the women next scraped the remaining flesh from the skin, then stretched and dried it in the sun to make a stiff leather called rawhide. To soften the leather, they worked the brains of the animal into the rawhide. After the skin had dried, they rubbed and stretched the leather until it became soft and pliant. Women fashioned rawhide into storage pouches called parfleches and the soft leather into bags, blankets, and clothing.

Men usually wore buckskin breechcloths drawn between the legs and tied around the waist, leaving a flap hanging down in the front and back. They draped buckskin ponchos over their shoulders and wore buckskin leggings and moccasins with rawhide soles to protect their ankles and calves from cactus and jagged rocks. The eastern Apaches wore the Plains-style low-cut moccasins while the western tribes turned down their tall moccasins at the knee to make a pocket for carrying knives and other objects. Men usually wore their hair at shoulder length and tied a cloth headband across the forehead.

Traditionally, women wore buckskin skirts, along with ponchos and moccasins like the men. They generally wore their hair long, although unmarried Western Apache women shaped their hair into an hourglass-shaped roll tied with a bow. Both women and men

After contact with the Pueblos and the Spanish, women began to favor long cloth dresses and shawls, along with ornate jewelry.

shampooed their hair with aloe. The roots of this plant were collected and pounded into a pulp, placed in water, and worked into a sudsy lather. The hair was then combed with a short bunch of stiff grass tied into a firm bundle.

The Apaches obtained cloth and wool from the Pueblos and other tribes. It was not until the early 1900s, however, that most men began to adopt Euro-American styles, including white cotton shirts, cartridge belts, and black vests. During this time, women came to favor long-sleeved cotton blouses and full skirts. The dresses were plain or calico, edged with a wide ruffle at the bottom. In later years, many women also began to wear numerous strands of beads around their necks from which mirrors, shells, bear claws, colored Mexican beans, and other medicine tokens were hung. They also liked earrings made of pieces of iridescent shell from the Pacific coast, as well as brass or silver bracelets.

During ceremonies, the Apache continue to wear traditional clothing. During her puberty rite, the Sunrise Ceremony, a girl dons a two-piece buckskin dress of the highest quality. Her fringed dress is adorned with shells, beads, and little pieces of metal. When leading ceremonies the medicine man wears a buckskin garment decorated with feathers, beads, and paint that indicate his spiritual powers.

Handicrafts

Along with making wickiups and buckskin clothing, women were highly skilled at many handicrafts, including pottery and basket making. They made deerskin storage bags, which they dyed brown

Apache women have long made different kinds of baskets for storing water and carrying food and belongings.

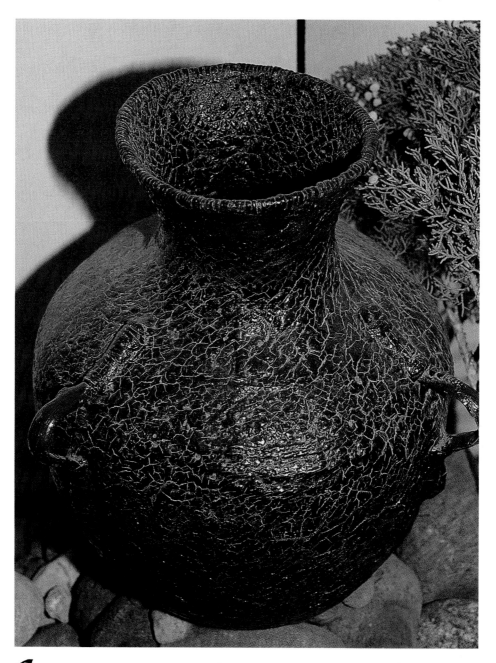

Storage jars had countless uses for the Apache. A coating of pitch ensured the vessel was watertight and could hold both liquids and dry goods.

with walnut hulls. Gourds were fashioned into cups while plates, spoons, and awls came from bones and wood. Handmade pots were usually gray or brown with rounded bases and flared rims. These pots did not need to have flat bottoms because they are placed on the sandy ground, not on tabletops. The Apache used the pots as cooking vessels. However, they did not have many pots since they could be easily broken during their travels. Of all their talents, the Apache were most skilled at basket making. Using both coiling and twining, they made many kinds of baskets decorated with geometric and animal designs using vegetable dyes. Light and portable, baskets were used for storage, sifting, and gathering.

Women wove four different types of baskets: trays and bowls, storage jars, carrying or burden baskets, and water jars coated with pitch. The most common were trays and bowls, ranging from 4 to 30 inches in diameter and with flared sides. These were used for many tasks—serving and boiling food, holding flour, sifting seeds, crushing berries, and parching corn. Tapering to a small neck with a wide rim, tall jars were used for storing dry goods. These baskets were fashioned by coiling thin cottonwood or willow splints over a base of three peeled branches. Women decorated their baskets and jars with black geometric designs, which stood out against the tan color of the splints.

The Apaches made large burden or carrying baskets from split sumac or willow twigs in a technique called twining. They decorated the wide-mouthed baskets with three or four bold horizontal bands and fringed them with strips of buckskin, or in more recent years with tin cones or pendants. Water jars were essential in the desert country where water was scarce. The jars could be large or small, with a narrow neck and a leather handle on each side. To make these jars women wove strips of split sumac. Sometimes they rubbed red ocher over the jar to fill in the spaces in the weave and to create a striking design. Then, with a stick to which they had attached a scrap of buckskin or a piece of shredded yucca, they coated the inside of the jar and occasionally the outside with melted piñon pitch.

Most Apache baskets were similar in shape, but the designs of each tribe could be distinctive. The Jicarilla were known for their small baskets, which served as drinking cups, while the Western Apaches made black-and-tan baskets with small coils and a fine, even weave. Both the Chiricahua and Mescalero often used yucca leaves, which gave their baskets a light green or brown color.

Apache men crafted weapons for hunting, raiding, and warfare. They made bows, which were 3 to 4 feet long, from mulberry, oak, or locust wood. They first cut, smoothed, and seasoned the wood, then bent and tied the bow, which was finally placed in hot ashes. When the bow was removed and cooled, it retained its curved shape. Sometimes, they backed the bow with sinew for added strength. Men painted solid colors on the outer edge and designs on the inside of the curve of the bow. They made the bowstrings from split deer or buffalo sinew twisted together into a strong cord. To make arrows, they simply fire-hardened the tips of wooden shafts, although the Western Apache and Chiricahua favored canes or reeds, which they fitted with a hardened foreshaft of mulberry or mountain mahogany.

*I*n addition to geometric designs, Apache basket makers decorated their creations with the figures of people and animals as well.

Men made their own stone points or picked up arrowheads at ancient ruins and tied them to the shafts. About 30 inches long, arrows were fletched with the split tail or wing feathers of eagles, buzzards, or red-tailed hawks attached with sinew or piñon pitch. The shafts were then painted with red or black bands. The Apache also made quivers and bow covers from mountain lion hides, including the fur and tail, although deer, pronghorn, and wildcat skins were also used. They also made war clubs, hide shields, and lances with fire-hardened tips, as well as stone knives.

Storytelling

Apache stories instructed and entertained young and old alike. Held sacred, these stories explained the creation of the universe, the origin of the Apache, and the mysteries of nature. Others, such as the adventures of Coyote and Big Owl, amused people as well as offered lessons. Coyote was honored as a hero, because he taught the Apaches how to survive in the often harsh terrain of the Southwest. He also showed them how to plant corn, weave baskets, and most impotantly how to build a strong society. Yet he could also be a mischievous character who made foolish decisions, and then had to suffer the consequences. In other words, just like people, he had many flaws.

Here is a Chiricahua Apache story about how Coyote brought fire to the world, which the people desperately needed for cooking and keeping warm on cold winter nights.

In this Edward Curtis photograph, entitled Story-telling—Apache, *several people gather around an older man relating a tale of the past.*

"Coyote Steals Fire from the Birds"

In the beginning only the birds had fire. They kept the fire in a secret place and would not share it with others.

One day, Coyote wandered to where the birds' children were shooting arrows. He began to play with the little ones beside the bluff, and he quickly won all their arrows in the shooting contest.

"Do you know the path to that bluff? I know the way," he said to the children. He didn't really know how to get there, but he wanted to steal the fire and hoped to trick one of the little birds into telling him how to get to it.

The young birds answered, "Our parents told us not to tell anyone."

"I'll give half these arrows to anyone who can tell me how to get up that bluff," Coyote declared.

Although the little birds wanted their arrows back, they again refused. So, Coyote offered them all the arrows, and the youngest bird blurted, "See that piñon tree on the edge of the bluff. If you tell that piñon to bend down, it will lift you up to the bluff."

Coyote gave half the arrows to the bird. He wanted to make sure he was telling the truth before giving up all of them. He told the piñon tree to bend down, and it did so. Then the tree carried Coyote up to the bluff where the birds made their home. He met the birds and told them he had exciting news. "All your enemies throughout the country have been killed!" he cried. "Let us have a great celebration tonight!"

The birds were delighted with this news. That evening they came together, making four large rings for each of the different kinds of birds.

When no one was looking, Coyote slipped away and stripped off the soft bark of the juniper tree, which he tied under his tail. Then he returned and joined in the dance, making sure he got close to the fire. Every now and then he stuck his tail into the orange and yellow flames as the others were enjoying the celebration.

One of the birds told Coyote, "Old one, you're going to burn your tail."

"Let it burn!" Coyote cried joyously. "I feel so happy that all our enemies have been killed. That is why I am acting this way."

But some of the birds quickly became suspicious. "Friends, he is trying to get away with our fire," they said.

"No, no," Coyote assured them, "I'm just celebrating."

He stuck his tail into the fire one more time, leaving it there long enough for the juniper bark to ignite. Then Coyote ran away into the night.

The birds were not able to catch him, so they begged Wasp and Hawk to make the rain fall. But as the torrents came down upon him, Coyote gave the fire to Bumblebee who sheltered the flames in a hole in a tree.

After the downpour, Coyote shared the fire with all the creatures of the earth, which is how people acquired fire. The Chiricahua say it is also why Coyote's tail is now scorched yellow underneath and burned black at the tip.

Raiding and Warfare

During the seventeenth century, bands of Apache raiders roved the land, often sweeping as far south as Jalisco, Mexico. Some Apaches, most likely Jicarillas and Mescaleros, traded with the Pueblo Indians of New Mexico, exchanging hides, tallow, and captives for cotton cloth, tobacco, and food. Instead of trading, however, most Apaches, in parties of four to twelve men, preferred to raid Pueblo villages, as well as the camps of other native peoples. They stole horses, corn, and goods and kidnapped women and children. Later, they attacked Spanish, Mexican, and Anglo settlements in a similar fashion.

Although the Apache struck terror in their victims, they viewed raiding simply as a means of providing for themselves, like hunting and gathering. They could have completely destroyed all the villages in the Mexican provinces of Sonora and Chihuahua, but they needed the inhabitants to continue to raise livestock and crops for them to steal. They preferred to quietly slip into villages in the early morning, sieze livestock or food, and leave without a trace. Masters of deception, they could seemingly blend into the rocks and brush around them. They often raided a village and vanished before anyone realized what had happened. Then the raiders might ride or run hard, going without sleep for four or five days until they were certain they were not being pursued. They had remarkable strength and endurance—a man on foot could run seventy miles a day. When they arrived back at their camp they were expected to share their plunder among everyone.

In Fresh Trail Apache War Party, *a 1952 painting by Allan Houser, a group of warriors charges across the desert on their spirited horses.*

An Apache might recite this chant when he wished to hide from his pursuers:

> *Right here in the middle of this place*
> *I am becoming Mirage*
> *Let them not see me,*
> *For I am of the sun.*

The Apache usually went to war to avenge a wrong—they often fought among themselves. If one Apache killed another, the maternal relatives of the slain were obligated to avenge his death. If a Mexican or Anglo killed an Apache, even if he had been stealing horses, the chief of his band or clan raised a war party against the enemy. War parties might have as many as two hundred men, including a medicine man who predicted the outcome of the conflict.

Everyone who wished to join the war party came together in a "going-to-war" ceremony. In preparing for battle, they called upon the supernatural, which they referred to as "the enemies against power." They believed this force allowed them to surprise and quickly defeat their foe. It could raise a strong wind and clouds of dust to conceal them or make their horses easy to handle during the attack. The great leader Geronimo and some Apache women also believed that this force gave them the power to know what was happening far away.

On the warpath the Apache were intent on killing the enemy or any of the enemy's people. If they captured an adult male, he was handed over to the women in the dead Apache's family to be killed. Captured children were usually adopted into the band.

Masters of the surprise attack, the Apache preferred a guerilla style of warfare. With only a few thousand people, including women and children in each of the divisions, they could not afford to lose many people in pitched battles. They scorned heroics, favoring stealth over open warfare. "I am calling on the sky and earth," warriors chanted. "Bats will fly and turn upside down with me in battle. Black sky will enfold my body and give me protection, and earth will do the same."

The Apaches, despite their small numbers, were determined to keep their freedom. They ably resisted all efforts to conquer them, often by much larger forces, from the seventeenth century to the last years of the nineteenth century. Even then, they had to be tracked by their own people or they might never have been caught.

To this day,
people dance to
the rhythm of drums at
the Sunrise Ceremony, which
stands at the heart of Apache beliefs.

THE TRADITIONAL RELIGION OF THE APACHES INCLUDES MANY DIVINE spirits, the most prominent being White Painted Woman, also known as Changing Woman, and her twin sons Slayer of Monsters and Child Born of Water. Among the Apache, the sky, earth, sun, and moon are spirits, as are the Water People and the Mountain Spirits, known to the Western Apache as Gan. The Gan, who inhabit caves hidden in the rocky slopes, once lived as people but became spirits in search of eternal life. Like other native peoples, the Apache religion was part of daily life. It aided in hunting, gathering, and farming, as well as protected them from injury and illness.

The Apache dreaded any kind of ailment—either physical or spiritual. If a disease struck their camp, they fled in panic. They also believed the worst maladies were borne by creatures, especially owls, bears, and coyotes. Such illnesses had to be treated by a shaman, or medicine man, who had acquired special powers from these animals. The Apache especially dreaded owls, and the appearance of one of these birds around camp aroused great concern. There were no jokes and few stories about owls, because it was considered bad luck to even mention the bird's name.

The Apache greatly feared ghosts and witches as well. Ghosts were believed to be the souls of the dead—most of whom were sinister. They might chase or throw rocks at people, or play other harmless tricks. If ghosts weren't treated properly, they could also bring misfortune and even death. Many people believed that ghosts rose from their graves and entered the bodies of owls. The hoot of an owl was the haunting voice of a ghost making threats against the

*L*ike many other cultures, the Apache believed the evening was the time when ghosts, witches, and sorcerers emerged to play tricks and work their evil on the living.

living. Anyone who heard the words would contract the owl sickness, which was believed to be fatal unless treated by a shaman whose powers came from owls.

Unlike ghosts, witches (or sorcerers among some Apache tribes) were thought to be living people who possessed magical, evil powers. Witches, or sorcerers, who could be men or women, worked mostly at night, often allying with evil spirits to harm others. Many Apache believed that all injuries and ills were brought on by their curses. People carried charms, such as turquoise beads, cattail pollen, and eagle feathers to ward off their evil influences. If they were the object of a witch's malice, they asked a medicine man to hold a special ceremony to cure them.

Medicine men had the power to heal both the body and the soul. They relied on songs, prayers, and sacred objects to remove a witch's spell and to cure the sick of ailments ranging from snakebite to arrow wounds. It was believed that supernatural power came only to those who searched for many years. Only then could one became a medicine man. These men diverted evil, foretold the future, and treated spiritual maladies, such as the deadly owl sickness. They also led ceremonies and sacred dances. These rituals, however, required the mastery of many elaborate chants in a language that differed from everyday Apache.

Although many Apache today practice Christianity, they also continue to believe in the old ways. Many people follow both religions in their communities on reservations in New Mexico and Arizona.

Ceremonies and Dances

Led by the medicine man, most Apache ceremonies had to do with healing the sick, preventing misfortune, or conducting puberty rites, although they might also be held to bring good fortune in hunting, the cultivation of crops, waging war, or rainmaking.

Among the most important is the Sunrise Ceremony in which a girl is welcomed into womanhood. It is believed that White Painted Woman initiated this ceremony in ancient times. The girl undergoing this rite is called by the name of this divine spirit during the four days and nights of the ritual and for four days afterward. Some Apache place the young woman in a ritual tipi. She traditionally wears a buckskin dress that has been dyed yellow—the color of sacred corn pollen—and decorated with symbols of the sun and moon. There are many rituals that make up the Sunrise Ceremony, including the molding ceremony in which the girl is massaged by a woman attendant to make her straight and supple. It is also believed that this ceremony will give her a good temperament. Sacred pollen is sprinkled, and the girl must drink through a straw so water does not touch her lips, which might result in the growth of unwanted facial hair. She must use a scratching stick instead of her fingernails to keep her skin unblemished. She also throws a blanket as a symbol of future wealth in each of the four directions, beginning with the east.

On the fourth morning, the ceremony often concludes with a footrace, the throwing of gifts, and the dismantling of the tipi. The young woman can then look forward to good health, prosperity, and

*F*acing the rising sun and with palms upraised, this young woman embarks on one of the most sacred and important rites, the Sunrise Ceremony.

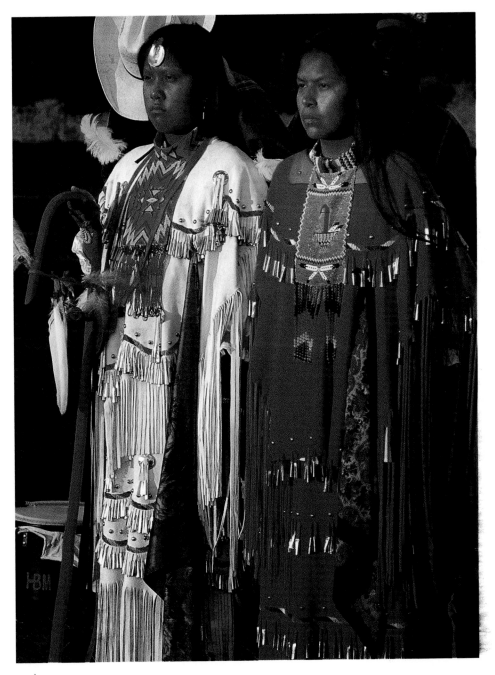

A young woman enlists her best friend for support during the four days and nights of the Sunrise Ceremony.

A basket holds fine grains of corn pollen, ready to be sprinkled during the Sunrise Ceremony.

a long life. Those who attend the ceremony also share in her blessings. It is believed that during the ceremony and for four days afterward, the young woman also possesses healing powers. She is then ready to marry and take her place in society.

There is feasting, dancing, and singing during the ceremonies, which are still held to this day. The medicine man recites long chants and ritually smokes. One of the most exciting events is the nightly performance of crown dancers representing the Gan, or Mountain Spirits. Four to sixteen dancers, along with a clown, dress in buckskin kilts and paint their entire bodies with black, yellow, and white designs. They wear striking masks with high, arching head-dresses and then dance by the light of the fire to bless the gathering and to drive away evil spirits. Here is a verse of one of the songs offered up by the medicine man as part of the ceremony:

In the middle of the Holy Mountain,
In the middle of its body, stands a hut,
Brush-built, for the Black Mountain Spirit.
White lightning flashes in these moccasins;
White lightning streaks in angular path;
I am the lightning flashing and streaking!
This headdress lives; the noise of its pendants
Sounds and is heard!
My song shall encircle these dancers!

5. Changing Ways

As they came into contact with European traders and settlers, the Apache began to adopt some styles of Western dress.

IT IS BELIEVED THAT THE ZUÑI WERE THE FIRST NATIVE PEOPLE OF THE Southwest to encounter the Spanish when Franciscan missionary Marcos de Niza arrived in 1539. A year later the Spanish explorer Francisco Vásquez de Coronado, searching for the legendary Seven Cities of Cíbola, journeyed northward from New Spain (now Mexico)

The Apache loved fine horses. Excellent riders, they often raided Pueblo and Spanish villages for new mounts.

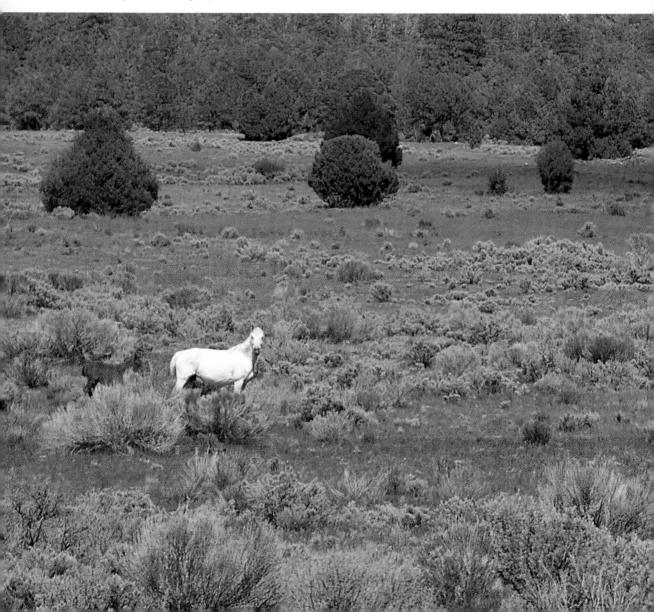

with a party of Spaniards and Indians. While visiting the western pueblos, inhabited by the Hopi and the Zuñi, as well as the northern New Mexico pueblos along the Rio Grande, he stole corn and cotton clothing. The party did not find any treasure and returned to Mexico, but the Spanish kept coming back. During their search for gold, the conquistadores took food and supplies from the peaceful inhabitants. If the people refused, they were severely punished or murdered.

Unlike the Pueblos who lived in villages, the Apaches avoided the Spanish by moving from place to place. The Jicarillas and Mescaleros were the first Apaches to directly encounter the Spanish when they met Francisco Vásquez de Coronado's expedition in western Texas and New Mexico in 1540. It was not until 1598, however, that the Apaches were forced to deal with the Spanish intrusion into their territory. In that year an expedition led by Juan de Oñate came into Pueblo country in the upper Rio Grande valley. Here, in present-day New Mexico, Oñate established a Spanish colony. Apaches first clashed with the Spanish in 1599 when they helped to defend Acoma Pueblo against an attack by Oñate. By 1610 the town of Santa Fe had been founded, and a few Apache bands, notably the Jicarilla, initially got along with the newcomers.

The Apache quickly learned the value of horses. Until the arrival of the Spanish, their only domesticated animal had been the dog. By trading and raiding, however, they acquired mounts and became expert horsemen. It is believed that by the 1630s Pueblos escaping Spanish enslavement had joined the Apaches and taught them how to ride horses. Like the Spanish, Apaches used braided ropes of horsehair and rawhide, saddles with wooden frames, stirrups, and cinch rings. For saddle blankets, they relied on deerskins, buffalo robes, or sheepskins.

Throughout the seventeenth century, the Spanish countered Apache raids on villages and travelers by capturing Apaches and selling them into slavery, often sending them south where they worked in mines. Yet the Apaches continued their raids, and during this time no village or road was safe. Herds of sheep, cattle, and livestock vanished in the night, forcing people to abandon entire villages. Apache raids left the cavalry unit at the presidio of Santa Fe horseless, so they couldn't ride after the attackers. Then the Apache, mostly Jicarillas and Mescaleros, as well as some Navajos, joined in the Pueblo Revolt of 1680. Led by the great Pueblo leader Popé, this union of Native Americans drove the Spanish completely out of New Mexico.

However, the Comanches had also acquired horses as they moved southward from present-day Wyoming. Quickly adapting to a plains way of life, they drove the Eastern Apaches—the most powerful and feared native people of the southern Plains—from the sprawling grasslands just as the Spanish were reconquering New Mexico in 1692. Settling in eastern New Mexico, where they could no longer hunt buffalo, the Eastern Apache also began to alternately trade with and raid the Spanish and other native peoples of the Southwest.

Conflicts continued with the Spanish for most of the 1700s. When the Spanish entered into a peace treaty with the Comanches in 1786, they engaged Comanche and Navajo warriors as troops to fight along with Spanish soldiers and to hunt down the Apache bands. The Spanish promised the Apaches provisions, if they agreed to settle near missions. Forced to cease their raids, some Apache bands lived peacefully with the Spanish until the Mexican Revolution, while others continued to make life hazardous for anyone who dared to venture into their lands.

The Apache Wars

When Mexico won independence from Spain in 1821, the Apache came under new, Mexican rulers. Although Mexico then governed the territory, including the present states of Arizona and New Mexico, it did not have enough soldiers to maintain effective control over the Apache. Then, in 1846, the United States declared war on Mexico and quickly took the land that would become the states of New Mexico, Arizona, Utah, Nevada, and California, as well as parts of Colorado and Wyoming. The Apache now found themselves under the authority of the United States government, but they still refused to surrender their homeland.

By the end of the Mexican-American War in 1848, the Apache had returned to raiding and warfare, often attacking Anglo homesteads. Known for their hostility, the Apache viewed these new settlers as intruders in their territory. United States officials, who did not understand the Apache, attempted to conquer the wandering people with brute military force. But the Apache, led by the great leaders Cochise and later Victorio, refused to be confined to reservations. During the 1870s, they resisted every effort to be subdued, as the United States embarked on what turned out to be a lengthy war in which they futilely pursued the Apache. The Apache Wars, as they came to be known, did not end until 1886, when Geronimo and his band finally surrendered and were sent to Florida, far from their ancestral home.

Sadly, at the end of this long conflict, many of the Apache were treated as prisoners of war. Removed from their homeland, they were

In Cochise's Wrath, *a 1951 painting by Will Sampson Jr., the great chief leads warriors against American soldiers.*

sent to Alabama and later Florida as well where they suffered terribly in the humid climate, finally ending up in Fort Sill, Oklahoma. Other Apaches were required to live on reservations in New Mexico and Arizona. During this time, many children were sent against their will to the Carlisle Indian School in Pennsylvania. In the 1890s, many Apaches were required to attend government and mission schools established on the reservations. Taught only in English, these schools attempted to coerce the Apaches to abandon their customs and heritage.

Forced onto reservations, the Apaches also suffered from poverty, malnutrition, and diseases, especially tuberculosis. By 1914, nine of every ten Jicarilla people were afflicted by this contagious disease. Between 1900 and 1920, one out of four people died. One of the reservation schools had to be turned into a tuberculosis sanitarium and was needed to treat patients until 1940.

Like other Native Americans, the Apache were not granted citizenship until 1924. They have since battled for their rights and the restoration of their homelands through legal means. In 1970, the Jicarilla Apache received nearly $10 million in compensation for lands taken from them, but they have not been able to win back any of this land. Over the course of this century, tribal leaders have vigorously worked to sustain the history, language, and customs of the Apache, notably through educational and cultural programs. They have also vigorously pursued economic independence and pioneered the Indian casino movement.

*T*hese Chiracahua Apache prisoners, including Geronimo (first row, third
from right), are about to begin their long journey of exile from their homeland.

A horse was a valuable tool in navigating the rugged western terrain.

Apache Language

The Apache languages belong to the Athapascan language family. There are four branches of this language family: Northern Athapascan, Pacific Coast Athapascan, Eyak, and Southwestern Athapascan. Sometimes called Apachean, Southwestern Athapascan includes seven separate though very closely related dialects: Navajo, Western Apache, Chiricahua, Mescalero, Jicarilla, Lipan, and Kiowa-Apache. Although all the dialects vary from one another, they share many words and can be understood by the different groups of Apaches.

Apache culture has been preserved through language. In fact, the different Apache groups have continued to speak their native tongue, which is even taught in public schools. You may wish to speak a few words of this fascinating language. They may appear a little difficult, but, if you follow this guide, you will gain some understanding of how words are pronounced in the Western Apache dialect.

The following examples are drawn from *Western Apache-English Dictionary* edited by Dorothy Bray in collaboration with the White Mountain Apache Tribe.

The vowels are pronounced as follows:

a	as in *father,*
e	as in *west*
i	as in *police*
o	as in *low*
u	as in *hut*

Double vowels like "aa" are pronounced the same, but the sounds are held a little longer. Some Apache words are nasalized, most of the air being expelled through the nose rather than the mouth, as in *m*, *n*, and *ng* in English. The vowels of these words usually have a hooked accent mark (a reversed, upside-down question mark under them, but are here indicated in boldface type). There is also a special kind of *l* intersected by a diagonal line (italicized here), which is voiceless, like a puff of air with the tongue in the "l" position. It is pronounced somewhat like the English "s*l*ip." The tone mark (') after a syllable means that you raise your voice when you say the syllable. The mark (') over a letter means that letter is stressed or emphasized, or that it is a glottal stop, as in *k'aa*, which is pronounced something like kuh-AH.

Some of the following words are especially important to Apache people. Others are everyday words.

apple	mansáána
arrow	k'aa'ist'aaní
bag	izis bena'iltiní
beans	bé'ísts'**ó**z
bear	shash
boy	ishkiin
cactus	hosh
canyon	hilwozh
chicken	tazhik'áné
desert	ni' dáá gos**g**ah
dog	gósé
eagle	itsá
egg(s)	iyéézh
father (my)	shitaa
father (his/her)	bitaa'
fire	k**o**'
firewood	chiizh

fish	lóg
girl	it'een
heat	gozdog
lightning	hách'ílgish
man	ndeen
meat	its**i**'
medicine	izee
moccasin	ké'igan
mother (my)	shimaa
mother (his)	b**aa**'
mountain	dzil
mouth	bizé'
no	dah
outdoors	da'idányú
owl	búh
prickly pear fruit	hoshcho
rabbit	gah
rawhide	ikágé
river	túnl**íí**'
school	óltag
shadow	bichagosh'oh
shirt	disis
shoe(s)	kee
snake	tł'iish
snare, trap	bee ijizhé
summer	sh**íí**
teacher	ilch'ígó'aahí
valley	bik**o**h
wagon	ts**i**naghái
warm (weather)	gozil
water	tú
winter	hai
woman	isdzán
yes	aa
yucca	igáyé

6. The Apache Today

Today, children
on the reservation
inherit two worlds—
the tradition of their
parents and ancestors and the
popular culture and technology
of the modern world.

TODAY, MANY APACHE LIVE ON RESERVATIONS IN ARIZONA, NEW MEXICO, and Oklahoma. The Western Apache make their home on the Fort Apache and San Carlos Reservations in east-central Arizona. The Chiricahua, who ranged in Arizona and New Mexico as well as Mexico, were removed from their own reservation in 1876 and imprisoned in Florida in 1886. Years later, some Chiricahua relocated to Oklahoma, where they still live, and others joined the Mescalero Apache in southern New Mexico. There are also Kiowa-Apaches in Oklahoma and Lipans in Texas. The Jicarilla have a reservation in northern New Mexico while Mescalero, Lipan, and many Chiricahua share the Mescalero Reservation.

Over the years, the Apache have proved themselves to be highly adaptable, even as they honor many of their traditional ways of life. When the Jicarilla formed a tribal government, most of the first tribal council members were medicine men or other traditional leaders. At least half the people on the reservation continue to speak the Jicarilla language and nearly three-quarters follow Apache religious beliefs. Yet today, fewer children are learning to speak the language of their parents and grandparents. So tribal leaders are using educational programs to help preserve their cultural heritage over the generations.

Most Apache in Arizona speak English. However, because many parents want their children to learn Apache as well, excellent bilingual programs have been established in the public schools on the San Carlos and Fort Apache Reservations. Schools are helping to provide vocational skills so that tribal members may stay on the reservation and earn a living. Tribal leaders reason that if people can

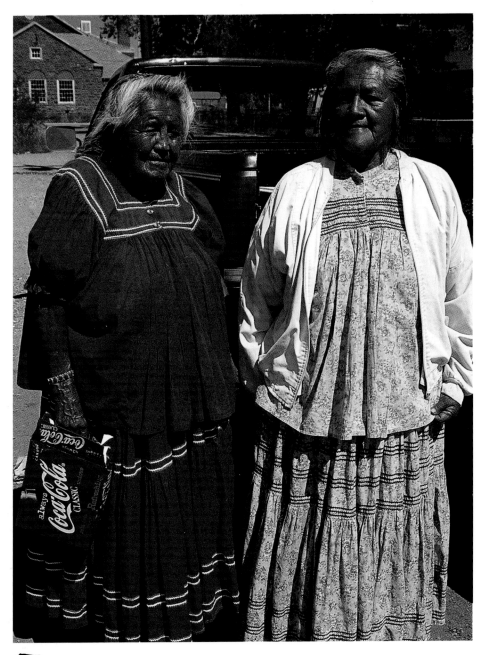

*T*hese women sell Apache burgers and sandwiches from the back of their pickup trucks at the "Tailgate Cafe" at Fort Apache, Arizona.

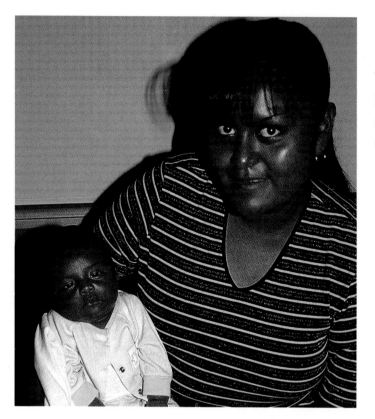

The next generation will learn the culture and traditions that have been passed on for centuries.

live within the community, Apache culture and social life are more likely to be sustained. Many people now work on farms and ranches, and the Apache have become well known as excellent rodeo competitors. Many men and women have also entered the professions as teachers, university professors, doctors, and artists, although they often must leave the reservations to pursue these fields.

Cattle, timber, and mining leases have become important sources of revenue on many reservations. A number of business enterprises also thrive on Apache reservations. The San Carlos cattle operation alone generates around a million dollars in sales annually. The Fort

Apache Timber Company, owned and managed by the White Mountain Apache in east-central Arizona, brings in more than $30 million a year and employs about four hundred Apache workers. Established by an Act of Congress in 1897, with a population of 13,000 people, this reservation also operates a popular ski resort, motel, and restaurant, and hosts the White Mountain Apache Tribal Fair and Rodeo. The annual event includes a parade, carnival, night dances, arts and crafts, and traditional sunrise dances.

Tourism, including hunting, fishing, and camping, has also become important to the economies of many reservation communities. Having once fought anyone who ventured into their homeland, the Apache now welcome visitors. Like the White Mountain Apaches, the Jicarilla and Mescalero Apaches operate ski resorts. The Mescalero operate the Inn of the Mountain Gods, a resort with a golf course, as well as horseback riding, tennis, and other recreational facilities. On their small reservation, the Yavapai Apache run a tourist complex at the Montezuma Castle National Monument.

Traditional crafts, including basket making and pottery, are being revived on many reservations. The Jicarilla have a gift shop where they sell baskets, beadwork, and fine buckskin items. Having fought other native peoples and droves of invaders, the Apache have long proved themselves to be vigorous survivors. Although they still face daunting social and economic problems, including unemployment and a shortage of adequate housing, the Apache are beginning to prosper in mainstream America without abandoning their heritage in the land that has been their home for centuries.

More About

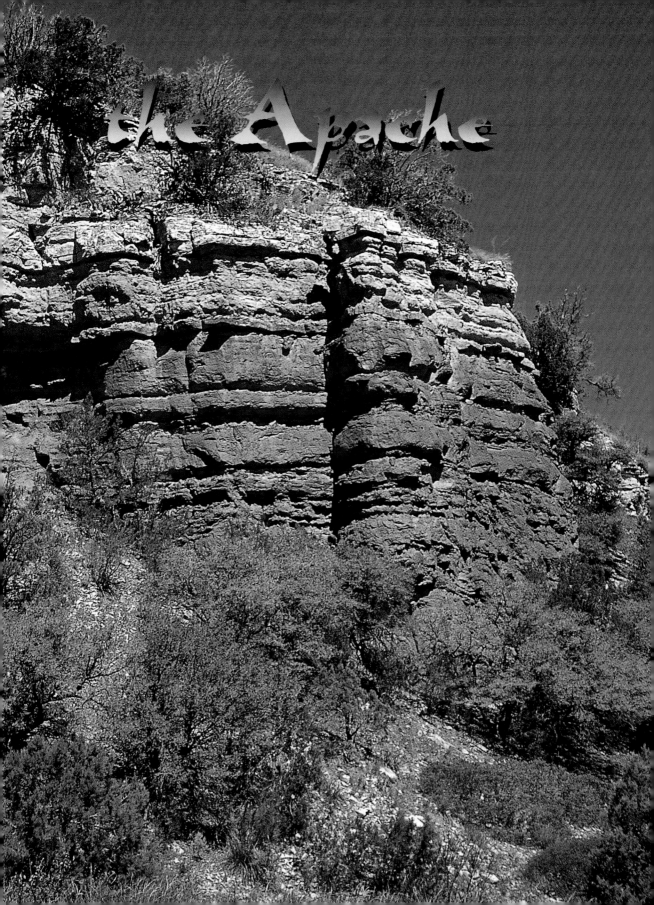

Time Line

10,000 B.C. First native peoples come to live in the American Southwest.

A.D. 1200–1400 Athapascan-speaking people (Apaches and Navajos) arrive in the Southwest.

1450 Another wave of migration scatters early Athapascan-speaking peoples throughout the Southwest.

1527 Four Spanish explorers from Pánfilo de Narváez's expedition travel into Apache territory.

about 1540 Francisco Vásquez de Coronado encounters the Apaches during his journey through the Southwest.

1598 Juan de Oñate claims New Mexico as a colony that is divided into governmental districts.

1610 Spain formally claims the entire Southwest, including Apache land, as a colony in the New World.

1600s Wandering Apache bands avoid capture and enslavement by Spanish colonists.

1700s Apaches continually war with the Spanish and Mexican invaders.

1821 Mexico wins independence from Spain and takes control of New Mexico, including Apache lands.

1824 The United States establishes the Bureau of Indian Affairs under the Department of War.

1829 Geronimo is born.

1830s Mexico offers a bounty for Indian scalps.

1848 The Mexican War concludes with the Treaty of Guadalupe Hidalgo, which cedes the Southwest, including Apache lands, to the United States.

1850s Forts are built in Apache territory.

1851 Mescalero and Jicarilla Apaches sign a peace treaty with James C. Calhoun, governor of New Mexico territory. After a severe beating, Mangas Coloradas goes on the warpath.

1858 Geronimo, a Chiracahua Apache, discovers that his mother, wife, and children have been murdered by Spanish troops from Mexico.

1861 War again breaks out between the Chiracahua Apache and the United States. Cochise eludes the U.S. Army and goes on the warpath.

1863 Mangas Coloradas is captured and beheaded. After his death, Cochise becomes principal chief.

1870 The U.S. government establishes reservations for the Apaches.

1871 Settlers massacre more than a hundred Apaches, mostly women and children, at Camp Grant.

1871–1872 Apaches are assigned to four reservations in the Southwest.

1872 Cochise signs a treaty with General Oliver Howard in which he agrees to end raids against settlers.

1874 Cochise dies of an unknown illness, and the Western Apaches are forced onto San Carlos Reservation.

1876 Refusing to live on a reservation, Geronimo flees to Mexico with his small band of Chiracahua Apaches.

1876–1886 Geronimo and his band fight in Arizona and Mexico to keep their freedom; Victorio is defeated at Tres Castillos in 1880; Geronimo finally surrenders to the U.S. Army in 1886.

1886–1894 The United States government exiles Apache bands to Alabama and then Florida, far from their homeland.

1894 Exiled Apaches, including Geronimo, are sent as prisoners to Fort Sill near present-day Lawton, Oklahoma.

1909 Geronimo dies at Fort Sill, Oklahoma.

1934 The Indian Reorganization Act recognizes tribal governments, beginning the process of self-government for the Apaches.

1940s Apaches seek compensation for land that was taken by the United States.

1970 Jicarilla Apaches receive $10 million from the Indian Claims Commission.

1982 The Jiracilla Apache win the right to tax minerals extracted from their land in the United States Supreme Court case *Merrion v. Jicarilla Apache Tribe*.

Notable People

Alchesay (Alchise) White Mountain Apache (active 1870s–1880s), was a sergeant in the Indian Scouts under the command of General George Crook, who took part in the Arizona campaign of 1872–1873 against the Apaches and Yavapais. In 1875 he received the Medal of Honor in recognition of his work. In 1886, he also helped Crook track down Geronimo, Chato, Kayatennae, and Mickey Free. Although he cooperated with the United States, he advocated fair treatment of his people. With Chato and Loco, he was a member of a delegation that met with President Grover Cleveland and other government officials. However, the delegates were unable to prevent the exile of the Apaches to Florida. Alchesay later became a successful cattle rancher.

Alchesay

Apache Kid (The Kid) Chiricahua Apache (about 1865–about 1894), army scout and outlaw, served in the U.S. Army under Al Sieber, chief of scouts in military campaigns against Geronimo during the 1880s. Sieber likely dubbed him "The Kid" and newspaper stories about his life as an outlaw later referred to him as "The Apache Kid." In 1887, Sieber left the Apache Kid in charge of the scouts at the San Carlos Agency. In his absence, the

Apache Kid and the scouts killed another Apache whom the young man suspected of murdering his father. When he returned, Sieber ordered the arrest of those involved, and a fight ensued. Sieber was wounded in the foot and the Apache Kid, along with several companions, escaped. Several weeks later they surrendered, and the Apache Kid was sentenced to seven years. But the small band escaped on their way to prison. All were captured or killed, except the Apache Kid who became one of the most notorious outlaws in Arizona. For years, he attacked settlers, taking their food, and many murders in the territory were attributed to him.

Mickey Free, one of the other Apache scouts, tracked the Apache Kid but never caught up with him. Finally, in 1894, an Apache woman said she had been with the Apache Kid as he lay dying in the mountains, most likely from tuberculosis. In 1897, Free claimed that he had found the remains of the Apache Kid in the mountains of New Mexico.

Chato (Alfred Chata or Chatto) Chiricahua Apache (about 1860–1934), leader and scout, escaped with Geronimo from the San Carlos Reservation in 1881. They hid out in the Sierra Madre in Mexico for about a year, then returned for several raids with Geronimo. In the early spring of 1883, while Geronimo and Chihuahua searched for livestock in Mexico, Chato led twenty-four warriors into Arizona. They were looking for ammunition and killed at least eleven settlers in several raids before heading back to Mexico. In retaliation, General George Crook attacked Chato's camp in Mexico. But the Apache warrior resisted. He and his band of sixty Apaches finally surrendered in February 1884. Geronimo surrendered a month later with his band of eighty Apaches.

In 1885, Geronimo fled from the reservation again. The following year, Chato helped General Crook track down Geronimo at Canyon de los Embudos in Mexico. However, in 1886, he also joined a delegation to Washington that demanded that the Apaches be allowed to remain in their homeland. Although he had helped the army, Chato was exiled to Florida with Geronimo and the other Apache prisoners. He lost his land and livestock at San Carlos. His children were later taken away from him and sent to the Carlisle Indian School.

In 1894, Chato, Geronimo, and other Apache exiles were moved to Fort Sill in Indian Territory, near present-day Lawton, Oklahoma. In 1913, he was at long last allowed to return to New Mexico, where he made his home on the Mescalero Reservation. He died many years later in an automobile accident.

Cochise ("Hardwood") Chiricahua Apache (about 1812–1874), leader, was falsely accused of kidnapping a child and rustling cattle from a ranch in 1861. The child grew up and became a famed army scout named Mickey Free. Lieutenant George Bascom led a troop of fifty soldiers to Apache Pass in the heart of the Chiricahua homeland. Setting up camp, Bascom requested a meeting with Cochise who arrived under a flag of truce with his family, including his son Naiche. Although Cochise insisted on his innocence, Bascom tried to arrest him. Wounded in the scuffle, Cochise slashed the tent with his knife and escaped. Bascom held many of the Apaches as hostages. In several raids, Cochise also captured several settlers. When negotiations failed, both the Apaches and the soldiers executed their hostages.

The Bascom Affair, as it came to be known, triggered the Apache Wars. Mimbrenos Apaches, under the leadership of Mangas Coloradas (Cochise's father-in-law), and Coyotero Apaches from the White Mountains joined Cochise. Their raids, especially during the Civil War when soldiers no longer manned the military posts, nearly drove Mexican and Anglo-American settlers from Arizona. In 1862, 3,000 California volunteers were brought in under the command of Colonel James H. Carleton. Cochise and Mangas Coloradas ambushed the troops at Apache Pass. Although the smaller band of Apaches held off the soldiers, Mangas Coloradas was wounded in the battle.

The following year, Mangas Coloradas was captured and killed by Carleton's troops, and Cochise became the leader of the Apache warriors.

Over the next decade, from a secret hideout in the Dragoon Mountains of southern Arizona, called the Stronghold, Cochise and his men swept down on settlers along the Butterfield Trail. Expert at deadly raids and quick escapes, Cochise was feared throughout the territory.

In 1871, Colonel George Crook took command of the army forces in Arizona. With the help of Indian scouts, he went after Cochise. After tracking down the famed leader, Crook negotiated a peace agreement, which Cochise rejected when he learned that his band would be sent to a reservation at Fort Tularosa, New Mexico. In the fall of 1872, General Oliver Howard, serving as President Ulysses S. Grant's representative, met with Cochise for eleven days. The general honored Cochise's request to live on a reservation near Apache Pass, and the great chief agreed to keep peace among his people. He remained true to his word until his death in 1874. His oldest son, Taza, who became chief, also kept the peace agreement, but upon Taza's death, Naiche, the younger son of Cochise, allied with Geronimo. By 1876, the Chiricahua Reservation was dissolved, and Apache raiders, led by Victorio and Geronimo, again terrorized the Arizona settlers.

Delshay Tonto Apache (about 1835–1874), leader, agreed that his band would live near Camp McDowell along the Verde River in Arizona and report occasionally to an Indian agent there. In 1871, following the massacre of Apaches at Camp Grant and an assault on Delshay by a soldier stationed at Camp McDowell, Delshay asked if his band could report to an agency in Sunflower Valley, which was closer to the homeland of the Tonto Apache. However, he received no answer.

A year later, in response to Western Apache raids, General George Crook embarked on the Tonto Basin Campaign. After several grueling battles, the troops surrounded Delshay's band. They surrendered and were taken to Fort Apache on the White Mountain Reservation of the Coyotero Apaches. Unhappy with their confinement, Delshay and his band moved from Fort Apache to Fort Verde along the Verde River. They were allowed to remain there as long as they did not attack settlers. They lived peacefully until they were joined by Apaches suspected of murdering Lieutenant Jacob Almy on the San Carlos Reservation.

Crook called for the arrest of Delshay who escaped into the Tonto Basin. For months, he artfully eluded the pursuing soldiers. Finally, Crook placed a bounty on him. In July 1874, an Apache brought in a head that he claimed was Delshay's. However, another Apache presented what he claimed was Delshay's head. Crook gave rewards to each of the men and displayed one head at Camp Verde and the other at the San Carlos Reservation.

Eskiminzin (Eskaminzin, Hackibanzin, "Angry Men Standing in Line for Him") Aravaipa-Pinal Apache (about 1825–1895), leader and peace advocate, was born a Pinal Apache, but married into the Aravaipas and became a leading chief. In 1871, as conflict between Apaches and settlers escalated, Eskiminzin met with Lieutenant Royal Whitman at Camp Grant near Tucson. He requested that his people be allowed to remain in their homeland, where the agave plant was their main food, instead of move to the White Mountain Reservation.

While Whitman sent the request to his superiors, the Apaches set up camp near the post. They planted cornfields, collected agave, and cut hay for the soldiers and settlers. However, raids in the spring of 1871 were blamed on Eskiminzin's band, and a gang of vigilantes under William Ouray attacked and killed about 150 members of Eskiminzin's band, mostly women and children. Outraged by the attack, President Ulysses S. Grant ordered a trial and offered to make peace with the Apaches. The vigilantes, however, were acquitted, and the Apaches intensified their raids.

Eskiminzin's people peacefully rebuilt their wickiups and replanted their fields. However in 1873, they were relocated sixty miles away to the San Carlos Reservation on the Gila River. When Lieutenant Jacob Almy was killed in an uprising of San Carlos Apaches the following summer Eskiminzin was mistakenly accused and arrested by General George

Crook. In January 1874, Eskiminzin escaped and led his band off the reservation. Months later, they returned, weary and hungry, and Eskiminzin was briefly jailed.

In 1886, Eskiminzin took part in peace negotiations in Washington, D.C. Taza, the son of Cochise and leader of the Chiricahua Apaches, died of pneumonia during the journey. He was succeeded by his younger brother, Naiche, who accused Eskiminzin of not taking proper care of Taza. To avoid a confrontation, Eskiminzin moved from the San Carlos Reservation and set up a ranch on the San Pedro River. When the ranch was destroyed by Anglo-Americans, Eskiminzin went back to the reservation. In 1888, he was arrested for simply associating with the Apache Kid who was married to Eskiminzin's daughter Chita. Eskiminzin was exiled to Florida with Geronimo and his Chiricahua Apaches. He was permitted to return to Arizona in 1889.

Mickey Free (Mig-ga-n'-la-iae) Pinal Apache (about 1847–1915), interpreter, scout, and tracker, was born in Mexico. His mother was Mexican and his father part Irish, as well as Pinalino. When he was about fourteen years old, he was kidnapped, which helped to trigger the Bascom Affair and the Apache resistance led by Cochise. He may have given himself the name "Mickey Free" to acknowledge his liberation from the Apaches.

At age fourteen, after he had been released, Mickey Free rescued the wife of an army captain from an attack by two Mexicans at Fort Bowie, Arizona, killing the men with a knife. When he was twenty Free became an interpreter and scout in the U.S. Army under George Stoneman. During the 1870s and 1880s, Free helped to track Geronimo through Arizona, New Mexico, and northern Mexico. During most of his career, Free served under chief of scouts, Al Sieber.

He also served as the official interpreter for the Chiricahua on the San Carlos Reservation. In 1886, he traveled to Washington, D.C., as interpreter for a delegation that included Chato, Loco, and Alchesay, and which sought to prevent the exile of Apaches to Florida. After this time, Free tracked the Apache Kid, as well as many outlaws. He claimed to have found the remains of the Apache Kid in 1897. He retired from the army in 1906.

Geronimo Chiracahua Apache (about 1825–1909), Apache leader, was born along the upper Gila River near present-day Clifton, Arizona. A full-blooded Chiricahua, he fought under Cochise and Mangas Coloradas. Although not a chief by birth, he proved his skill and courage in battle, especially against the Mexicans who had killed his mother, wife, and three children. Because of his great influence, he also came to be regarded as a medicine man.

In 1874, when Geronimo learned that the Chiricahuas were to be relocated from Apache Pass to the San Carlos Reservation, he and his followers escaped across the Mexican border into the Sierra Madre. He raided Mexican settlements and sold the stolen livestock to traders in New Mexico. When he visited the Warm Springs Reservation in New Mexico, Geronimo was arrested and taken to San Carlos where he remained until 1881. After conflict with army troops, he escaped the reservation with Juh, Naiche, Chato, and seventy-four other Apache to the mountains of Mexico. They returned to raid the reservation the following year, after which General George Crook was assigned to the Southwest to hunt down Geronimo and the defiant Apaches. With Apache scouts and trackers, they found and attacked Chato's camp, eventually convincing the leaders, including Geronimo, to return to San Carlos.

Geronimo and other leaders left the reservation again with about 150 Apaches in May 1885. They were tracked down by Crook's troops in March 1886, and agreed to return, but Geronimo and Naiche, along with twenty-four other Apaches, escaped on the way back. General Nelson Miles replaced Crook and he pursued Geronimo and his small band for months. Although he had 5,000 soldiers, he could not catch the elusive Geronimo. On September 4, 1886, Geronimo and his followers surrendered for the last time at Canyon de los Embudos, about 65 miles south of Apache Pass.

Geronimo

Along with hundreds of other Apaches, Geronimo was sent by railroad to prison in Florida. About a year later, some of the Apaches, including Geronimo, were moved to Alabama. Many died of tuberculosis and other diseases in the humid climate. Geronimo and the other Chiricahuas were never allowed to return to their homeland. In 1894, they accepted an offer from the Kiowas and Comanches to share their reservation near Fort Sill in present-day Oklahoma. Geronimo farmed there and wrote his memoirs. When he died in 1909, he was still considered a prisoner of war.

Allan Houser Chiricahua Apache (1914–1994), acclaimed sculptor, was born near Apache, Oklahoma. In the 1960s, he became a charter faculty member of the Institute of American Indian Arts in Santa Fe, New Mexico, where he cast bronze statues and taught until 1975. Thereafter, he devoted himself to creating bronze, stone, and wood sculptures. He was best known for large sculptures, and his work is today included in the collections of the Metropolitan Museum of Art, the Heard Museum, the Denver Art Museum, and the Fine Arts Museum of the University of New Mexico, among others.

Houser received many awards for his work, including the Prix de West Award in 1993 for a bronze sculpture entitled *Smoke Signals*. One of his most famous works, a bronze statue of an Indian woman entitled *As Long as the Waters Flow*, today stands in front of the state capitol in Oklahoma City. In 1994, he presented an eleven-foot bronze sculpture to First Lady Hillary Rodham Clinton as a gift from Native Americans to all people.

Mangas Coloradas Mimbreno Apache (about 1797–1863), Apache leader, father-in-law of Cochise, lived in the Mimbres Mountains in southwestern New Mexico. After Mexican officials offered a bounty for Apache scalps and many people were murdered, Mangas Coloradas united several bands under his leadership. They raided until the United States took over New Mexico Territory. In 1846, he signed a peace treaty with General Stephen Watts Kearny. However, conflicts arose over the return of Mexican captives and the murder of an Apache that went unpunished. There were further conflicts when miners passed through the region during the California Gold Rush of 1849. Mangas Coloradas intensified his raids on settlers and travelers along the Butterfield Trail.

In the early 1860s, when soldiers left the forts in Apache country to fight in the Civil War, California governor John Downey sent volunteers to protect the route through Arizona. In 1862, the Chiricahuas under Cochise and the Mimbrenos under Mangas Coloradas attacked the advance column at Apache Pass. Mangas Coloradas was shot in the chest and taken to Mexico where a doctor was ordered to care for him. After he recovered, he continued to raid until General Joseph West sought a meeting with him under a flag of truce. However, when he arrived at the army camp, he was taken prisoner and sent to Fort McLane on the Mimbres River. General West apparently wanted the leader to be killed and two sentinels shot Mangas Coloradas, claiming he had tried to escape.

Upon the death of Mangas Coloradas, Cochise became the principal chief of his band in the Apache Wars.

Naiche (Natchez, Nachi, Nache) Chiricahua Apache (about 1857–1921), son of Cochise, and grandson of Mangas Coloradas, was a leader during conflicts with U.S. forces in the late 1800s. He was with his father during the Bascom Affair and was briefly held hostage. His father taught him to remain loyal to his brother Taza. When Taza died unexpectedly of pneumonia in 1876, Naiche, whose name means "the Mischief Maker," led raiding parties. A hereditary chief, Naiche was a close ally of Geronimo in the Apache Wars. In 1879, he resisted relocation on the San Carlos Reservation and fled to Mexico with Geronimo's band. After years of conflict with U.S. military forces, he finally surrendered with Geronimo in 1886. Relocated and imprisoned at Fort Marion, Florida, in 1894 he was moved to Fort Sill in present-day Oklahoma along with other Apaches, including Geronimo. Naiche was not permitted to return to his homeland in Arizona until 1913. Eight years later, he died of influenza.

Naiche and wife

Victorio Mimbreno Apache (about 1825–1880), leader, was likely born in southern New Mexico. As a young man, Victorio fought under Mangas Coloradas. When the great Mimbreno chief died in 1863, Victorio became a leader of his and other Apache bands. This group, which included Mimbreno, Mogollon, Copper Mine, Chiricahua, and Mescalero, became known as the Ojo Caliente, or Warm Springs, Apaches, after the location of their agency in southwestern New Mexico.

During the 1860s and 1870s, the Warm Springs Apaches frequently raided in New Mexico and Texas. Victorio offered to stop the attacks if his people were given a permanent reservation. However, he and his followers were forced to move to the San Carlos Reservation where they lived with the Chiricahuas. In 1877, Victorio and about three hundred followers escaped, but most surrendered within a month at Fort Wingate, New Mexico. Victorio and about eighty warriors hid out in the Mimbres Mountains and occasionally raided settlements in the region. At the beginning of 1879, he attempted to settle at Warm Springs again, but in June he agreed instead to move to the Mescalero Reservation at Tularosa, New Mexico. Indicted on a charge of murder and horse theft, he fled with several warriors and a number of Mescaleros. They attacked a cavalry camp, killing eight soldiers, then went to Mexico. As they wandered into Texas, back into New Mexico, and then Arizona, they engaged in a series of raids.

While fleeing American soldiers in October 1880, Victorio and his followers were attacked by Mexican and Tarahumara Indians. During the two-day battle of Tres Castillos about eighty Apaches were killed and almost as many women and children taken prisoner. Only about thirty warriors escaped—but not Victorio. He was found among the dead, either killed by a Tarahumara or having taken his own life.

Nana became leader of his band, joining Geronimo in the Apache Wars of the 1880s.

Victorio

Glossary

Apachería   Spanish name for Apache lands. Also sometimes called Grand Apachería.

Athapascan   language family of the Apaches and Navajos and many native peoples of western Canada and Alaska.

bear grass   grassy plant used to thatch wickiups.

canyon   a deep valley, usually fairly narrow, with steep, rocky walls on either side.

Chiricahua   an Apache people now living in New Mexico and Oklahoma.

cradleboard   wooden board used to carry a baby.

Four Corners   common name for the place where the borders of Utah, Colorado, Arizona, and New Mexico come together.

Gan   Mountain Spirits; also the name of the Mountain Spirit Dancers, or Crown Dancers.

Hactcin   Spirit powers; creators of the world in the Jicarilla Apache origin story.

Jicarilla   an Apache people now living in New Mexico.

mesa   a hill or mountain with steep vertical sides and a flat top like a table.

Mescalero   an Apache people now living in Arizona; the name refers to the mescal plant, gathered for food.

Ndee   name the Apache use for themselves, meaning "the people." Also N'de and Ndé.

plateau   high, flat land.

shaman   medicine man who led all Apache religious ceremonies.

Western Apache   people living in Arizona, including White Mountain Apache, San Carlos Apache, Northern Tonto, and Southern Tonto.

wickiup   dome-shaped shelter made of saplings and brush used by the Apaches.

Further Information

Readings

Many impressive books have been written about the Apaches. Among them, the following titles were very helpful in researching and writing this book.

"The Origin of the Jicarilla Apache" and "Coyote Steals Fire from the Birds" are adapted from stories collected by Morris Edward Opler and published in *Memoirs of the American Folklore Society*.

Baldwin, Gordon C. *The Apache Indians: Raiders of the Southwest*. New York: Four Winds Press, 1978.

Basso, Keith H., and Opler, Morris Edward. *Apachean Culture History and Ethnology*. Tucson: University of Arizona Press, 1971.

Debo, Angie. *Geronimo: The Man, His Time, His Place*. Norman: University of Oklahoma Press, 1976.

Encyclopedia of North American Indians. Tarrytown, NY: Marshall Cavendish, 1997.

Forbes, Jack D. *Apache, Navaho, and Spaniard*. Norman: University of Oklahoma, 1994.

Goodwin, Grenville. *Western Apache Material Culture: The Goodwin and Guenther Collections*. Tucson: University of Arizona by University of Arizona Press, 1996.

Johansen, Bruce E., and Grinde, Donald A. Jr. *The Encyclopedia of Native American Biography*. New York: Henry Holt and Co., 1997.

Langer, Howard J. ed. *American Indian Quotations*. Westport, CT: Greenwood Press, 1996.

Mails, Thomas E. *The People Called Apache*. Englewood Cliffs, NJ: Prentice-Hall, 1974.

Malinowski, Sharon. *Notable Native Americans.* Detroit: Gale Research, 1995.

Malinowski, Sharon, and Sheets, Anna. *The Gale Encyclopedia of Native American Tribes.* Detroit: Gale Research, 1998.

Ortiz, Alfonso. *Handbook of North American Indians*, Volume 10, Southwest. Washington, D.C.: Smithsonian Institution, 1983.

Roberts, David. *Once They Moved Like the Wind: Cochise, Geronimo, and the Apache Wars.* New York: Simon & Schuster, 1994.

Swan-Jackson, Alys. *The Apaches and Apache Peoples of the Southwest.* Oxford: Heinemann, 1996.

Sweeney, Edwin R. *Cochise: Chiricahua Apache Chief.* Norman: University of Oklahoma, 1995.

Tiller, Veronica E. Velarde. *The Jicarilla Apache Tribe: A History.* Lincoln: University of Nebraska Press, 1992.

Waldman, Carl. *Encyclopedia of Native American Tribes.* New York: Facts on File, 1988.

———. *Who Was Who in Native American History: Indians and Non-Indians from Early Contacts through 1900.* New York: Facts on File, 1990.

Wilson, Chesley Goseyun. *When the Earth Was Like New: Western Apache Songs and Stories.* Danbury, CT: World Music Press, 1994.

Worcester, Donald Emmet. *The Apaches: Eagles of the Southwest.* Norman: University of Oklahoma Press, 1979.

Wyckoff, Lydia L. *Visions and Voices: Native American Painting from the Philbrook Museum of Art.* Tulsa, OK: The Philbrook Museum of Art, 1994.

Young people who wish to learn more about the Apaches will enjoy these excellent books for children:

Aleshire, Peter. *Reaping the Whirlwind: The Apache Wars.* New York: Facts On File, 1998.

Claro, Nicole. *The Apache Indians.* New York: Chelsea House, 1992.

Doherty, Craig A. *The Apaches and Navajos*. New York: Franklin Watts, 1989.

Fleischner, Jennifer. *The Apaches: People of the Southwest*. Brookfield, CT: Millbrook Press, 1994.

Geronimo and the Apache Indians. Peterborough, NH: Cobblestone Publishing, 1996.

Hermann, Spring. *Geronimo: Apache Freedom Fighter*. Springfield, NJ: Enslow, 1997.

Holt-Goldsmith, Diane. *Apache Rodeo*. New York: Holiday House, 1995.

Lacapa, Kathleen. *Less Than Half, More Than Whole*. Flagstaff, AZ: Northland, 1994.

Lacapa, Michael. *Antelope Woman: An Apache Folktale*. Flagstaff, AZ: Northland, 1992.

———.*The Flute Player: An Apache Folktale*. Flagstaff, AZ: Northland Pub., 1990.

Lund, Bill. *The Apache Indians*. Mankato, MN: Bridgestone Books, 1998.

McCall, Barbara A. *The Apaches*. Vero Beach, FL: Rourke Publications, 1990.

Schwarz, Melissa. *Cochise, Apache Chief*. New York: Chelsea House, 1992.

———. *Geronimo: Apache Warrior*. New York: Chelsea House, 1991.

Sneve, Virginia Driving Hawk. *The Apaches*. New York: Holiday House, 1997.

Organizations

Apache Business Committee
P. O. Box 1220
Anadarko, OK 73005
(405) 247-9493

Apache Tribe of Fort Sill
Route 2, Box 121
Apache, OK 73006
(405) 588-2298

Fort McDowell Mohave-Apache Council
P. O. Box 17779
Fountain Hills, AZ 85268
(602) 990-0995

Jacarilla Apache Tribal Council
P. O. Box 147
Dulce, NM 87528
(505) 759-3242

Mescalero Apache Tribal Council
P. O. Box 176
Mescalero, NM 88340
(505) 671-4495

San Carlos Tribal Council
P. O. Box 0
San Carlos, AZ 85550
(602) 475-2361

Tonto Apache Tribal Council
Tonto Reservation #30
Payson, AZ 85541
(602) 474-5000

White Mountain Apache Tribal Council
P. O. Box 700
Whiteriver, AZ 85941
(602) 338-4346

Yavapai-Apache Community Council
P. O. Box 1188
Camp Verde, AZ 86322
(602) 567-3649

Websites

Native Americans have created many websites on the Internet. Here are some of the most interesting sites to visit for more information about the Apache and visiting their reservations.

Apaches: Jicarilla, Mescalero, and Chiricahua
http://gonewmexico.miningco.com/msubapch.htm

The Children of Changing Woman (Peabody Museum)
http://www.peabody.harvard.edu/maria/Cwoman.html

Cradleboard Elementary School
http://www.cybertrails.com/~azboater/index.html

Geronimo: His Own Story
http://odur.let.rug.nl/~usa/B/geronimo/geronixx

Jicarilla Apache Tribe
http://www.jade2.tec.nm.us/

White Mountain Apache Tribe
http://www.wmat.nsn.us/

White Mountain Apache Tribe
http://www.primenet.com/~itca/Tribes/whitemtn.htm

Yavapai-Apache Nation
http://www.yavapai-apache-nation.com/

Index

Raymond Bial

HAS PUBLISHED MORE THAN THIRTY CRITICALLY ACCLAIMED BOOKS OF PHO-tographs for children and adults. His photo-essays for children include *Corn Belt Harvest, Amish Home, Frontier Home, Shaker Home, The Underground Railroad, Portrait of a Farm Family, With Needle and Thread: A Book About Quilts, Mist Over the Mountains: Appalachia and Its People, Cajun Home,* and *Where Lincoln Walked.*

He is currently immersed in writing *Lifeways,* a series of books about Native Americans. As with his other work, Bial's deep feeling for his subjects is evident in both the text and illustrations. He travels to tribal cultural centers, photographing homes, artifacts, and sur-roundings and learning firsthand about the national lifeways of these peoples.

A full-time library director at a small college in Champaign, Illinois, he lives with his wife and three children in nearby Urbana.